Connect
to Win

Dale Harbison Carnegie (November 24, 1888–November 1, 1955) was an American writer and lecturer and the developer of famous courses in self-improvement, salesmanship, corporate training, public speaking and interpersonal skills. Born into poverty on a farm in Missouri, he was the author of the bestselling *How to Win Friends and Influence People* (1936), *How to Stop Worrying and Start Living* (1948) and many more self-help books.

Connect to Win

Dale Carnegie's Guide to
Building Lasting Relationships

Dale Carnegie

RUPA

Published by
Rupa Publications India Pvt. Ltd 2024
7/16, Ansari Road, Daryaganj
New Delhi 110002

Sales centres:
Bengaluru Chennai
Hyderabad Jaipur Kathmandu
Kolkata Mumbai Prayagraj

P-ISBN: 978-93-5702-666-6
E-ISBN: 978-93-5702-761-8

Second impression 2024

10 9 8 7 6 5 4 3 2

Printed in India

CONTENTS

1

YOU CAN'T WIN AN ARGUMENT

Shortly after the close of World War I, I learnt an invaluable lesson one night in London. I was manager at the time for Sir Ross Smith. During the war, Sir Ross had been the Australian ace out in Palestine; and shortly after peace was declared, he astonished the world by flying halfway around it in 30 days. No such feat had ever been attempted before. It created a tremendous sensation. The Australian government awarded him $50,000; the King of England knighted him; and, for a while, he was the most talked-about man under the Union Jack. I was attending a banquet one night given in Sir Ross's honor; and during the dinner, the man sitting next to me told a humorous story which hinged on the quotation "There's a divinity that shapes our ends, rough-hew them how we will."

The raconteur mentioned that the quotation was from the Bible. He was wrong. I knew that. I knew it positively. There couldn't be the slightest doubt about it. And so, to get a feeling of importance and display my superiority, I appointed myself as an unsolicited and unwelcome committee of one to correct him. He stuck to his guns. What? From Shakespeare? Impossible! Absurd! That quotation was from the Bible. And he knew it.

The storyteller was sitting on my right; and Frank Gammond, an old friend of mine, was seated at my left. Mr.

Gammond had devoted years to the study of Shakespeare. So the storyteller and I agreed to submit the question to Mr. Gammond. Mr. Gammond listened, kicked me under the table, and then said: "Dale, you are wrong. The gentleman is right. It *is* from the Bible."

On our way home that night, I said to Mr. Gammond: "Frank, you knew that quotation was from Shakespeare."

"Yes, of course," he replied, "*Hamlet*, Act Five, Scene Two. But we were guests at a festive occasion, my dear Dale. Why prove to a man he is wrong? Is that going to make him like you? Why not let him save his face? He didn't ask for your opinion. He didn't want it. Why argue with him? Always avoid the acute angle." The man who said that taught me a lesson I'll never forget. I not only had made the storyteller uncomfortable, but had put my friend in an embarrassing situation. How much better it would have been had I not become argumentative.

It was a sorely needed lesson because I had been an inveterate arguer. During my youth, I had argued with my brother about everything under the Milky Way. When I went to college, I studied logic and argumentation and went in for debating contests. Talk about being from Missouri, I was born there. I had to be shown. Later, I taught debating and argumentation in New York; and once, I am ashamed to admit, I planned to write a book on the subject. Since then, I have listened to, engaged in and watched the effect of thousands of arguments. As a result of all this, I have come to the conclusion that there is only one way under high heaven to get the best of an argument—and that is to avoid it. Avoid it as you would avoid rattlesnakes and earthquakes.

Nine times out of ten, an argument ends with each of the contestants more firmly convinced than ever that he is absolutely right.

A BETTER LISTENER MAKES A BETTER PERSON

You can't win an argument. You can't because if you lose it, you lose it; and if you win it, you lose it. Why? Well, suppose you triumph over the other man and shoot his argument full of holes and prove that he is non compos mentis. Then what? You will feel fine. But what about him? You have made him feel inferior. You have hurt his pride. He will resent your triumph. And:

A man convinced against his will is of the same opinion still.

Years ago Patrick J. O'Haire joined one of my classes. He had had little education, and how he loved a scrap! He had once been a chauffeur, and he came to me because he had been trying, without much success, to sell trucks. A little questioning brought out the fact that he was continually scrapping with and antagonizing the very people he was trying to do business with. If a prospect said anything derogatory about the trucks he was selling, Pat saw red and was right at the customer's throat. Pat won a lot of arguments in those days. As he said to me afterward, "I often walked out of an office saying: 'I told that bird something.' Sure I had told him something, but I hadn't sold him anything."

My first problem was not to teach Patrick J. O'Haire to talk. My immediate task was to train him to refrain from talking and to avoid verbal fights.

Mr. O'Haire became one of the star salesmen for the White Motor Company in New York. How did he do it? Here is his story in his own words: "If I walk into a buyer's office now and he says: 'What? A White truck? That's no good! I wouldn't take one if you gave it to me. I'm going to buy the Whose-It truck,' I say, 'The Whose-It is a good truck. If you buy the Whose-It, you'll never make a mistake. The Whose-Its are made by a fine company and sold by good people.'

"He is speechless then. There is no room for an argument. If he says the Whose-It is best and I say sure it is, he has to stop. He can't keep on all afternoon saying, 'It's the best' when I'm agreeing with him. We then get off the subject of Whose-It and I begin to talk about the good points of the White truck.

"There was a time when a remark like his first one would have made me see scarlet and red and orange. I would start arguing against the Whose-It; and the more I argued against it, the more my prospect argued in favor of it; and the more he argued, the more he sold himself on my competitor's product.

"As I look back now I wonder how I was ever able to sell anything. I lost years of my life in scrapping and arguing. I keep my mouth shut now. It pays."

As wise old Ben Franklin used to say:

> If you argue and rankle and contradict, you may achieve a
> victory sometimes; but it will be an empty victory because
> you will never get your opponent's goodwill.

So figure it out for yourself. Which would you rather have, an academic, theatrical victory or a person's goodwill? You can seldom have both.

The Boston *Transcript* once printed this bit of significant doggerel:

> Here lies the body of William Jay, Who died maintaining
> his right of way—He was right, dead right, as he sped
> along. But he's just as dead as if he were wrong.

You may be right, dead right, as you speed along in your argument; but as far as changing another's mind is concerned, you will probably be just as futile as if you were wrong.

Frederick S. Parsons, an income tax consultant, had been disputing and wrangling for an hour with a government tax inspector. An item of $9,000 was at stake. Mr. Parsons claimed that this $9,000 was in reality a bad debt, that it would never be collected, that it ought not to be taxed. "Bad debt, my eye!" retorted the inspector. "It must be taxed."

"This inspector was cold, arrogant and stubborn," Mr. Parsons said as he told the story to the class. "Reason was wasted and so were facts... The longer we argued, the more stubborn he became. So I decided to avoid argument, change the subject, and give him appreciation.

"I said, 'I suppose this is a very petty matter in comparison with the really important and difficult decisions you're required to make. I've made a study of taxation myself. But I've had to get my knowledge from books. You are getting yours from the firing line of experience. I sometimes wish I had a job like yours. It would teach me a lot.' I meant every word I said.

"'Well.' The inspector straightened up in his chair, leaned back, and talked for a long time about his work, telling me of the clever frauds he had uncovered. His tone gradually became friendly, and presently he was telling me about his children. As he left, he advised me that he would consider my problem further and give me his decision in a few days.

"He called at my office three days later and informed me that he had decided to leave the tax return exactly as it was filed."

This tax inspector was demonstrating one of the most common of human frailties. He wanted a feeling of importance; and as long as Mr. Parsons argued with him, he got his feeling of importance by loudly asserting his authority. But as soon as his importance was admitted and the argument stopped and he was permitted to expand his ego, he became a sympathetic and kindly human being.

Buddha said: "Hatred is never ended by hatred but by love," and a misunderstanding is never ended by an argument but by tact, diplomacy, conciliation and a sympathetic desire to see the other person's viewpoint.

Lincoln once reprimanded a young army officer for indulging in a violent controversy with an associate. "No man who is resolved to make the most of himself," said Lincoln, "can spare time for personal contention. Still less can he afford to take the consequences, including the vitiation of his temper and the loss of self-control. Yield larger things to which you show no more than equal rights; and yield lesser ones though clearly your own. Better give your path to a dog than be bitten by him in contesting for the right. Even killing the dog would not cure the bite."

Opera tenor Jan Peerce, after he was married nearly fifty years, once said: "My wife and I made a pact a long time ago, and we've kept it no matter how angry we've grown with each other. When one yells, the other should listen—because when two people yell, there is no communication, just noise and bad vibrations."

POINTS TO REMEMBER

1. Proving someone wrong won't earn you any points.
2. The way to get the best of an argument is by avoiding it.
3. Even making one less enemy pays off.

THE BIG SECRET OF DEALING WITH PEOPLE

There is only one way under high heaven to get anybody to do anything. Did you ever stop to think of that? Yes, just one way. And that is by making the other person want to do it.

Remember, there is no other way.

Of course, you can make someone want to give you his watch by sticking a revolver in his ribs. You can make your employees give you cooperation—until your back is turned—by threatening to fire them. You can make a child do what you want it to do by a whip or a threat. But these crude methods have sharply undesirable repercussions.

The only way I can get you to do anything is by giving you what you want.

What do you want?

Sigmund Freud said that everything you and I do springs from two motives: the sex urge and the desire to be great.

John Dewey, one of America's most profound philosophers, phrased it a bit differently. Dr. Dewey said that the deepest urge in human nature is "the desire to be important". Remember that phrase: "the desire to be important." It is significant. You are going to hear a lot about it in this book.

What do you want? Not many things, but the few things that you do wish, you crave with an insistence that will not be denied. Some of the things most people want include:

1   Health and the preservation of life.
2   Food.
3   Sleep.
4   Money and the things money will buy.
5   Life in the hereafter.
6   Sexual gratification.
7   The well-being of our children.
8   A feeling of importance.

Almost all these wants are usually gratified—all except one. But there is one longing—almost as deep, almost as imperious, as the desire for food or sleep—which is seldom gratified. It is what Freud calls 'the desire to be great'. It is what Dewey calls the 'desire to be important'.

THE GREAT DESIRE

Lincoln once began a letter saying: "Everybody likes a compliment." William James said: "The deepest principle in human nature is the craving to be appreciated." He didn't speak, mind you, of the "wish" or the "desire" or the "longing" to be appreciated. He said the "craving" to be appreciated.

Here is a gnawing and unfaltering human hunger, and the rare individual who honestly satisfies this heart hunger will hold people in the palm of his or her hand and 'even the undertaker will be sorry when he dies.'

The desire for a feeling of importance is one of the chief distinguishing differences between mankind and the animals. To illustrate: When I was a farm boy out in Missouri, my father bred fine Duroc-Jersey hogs and pedigreed white-faced cattle. We used to exhibit our hogs and white-faced cattle at the country fairs and livestock shows throughout the Middle West. We won first prizes by the score. My father pinned his blue ribbons on a sheet of white muslin, and when friends or visitors came to the house, he would get out the long sheet of muslin. He would hold one end and I would hold the other while he exhibited the blue ribbons.

The hogs didn't care about the ribbons they had won. But Father did. These prizes gave him a feeling of importance.

If our ancestors hadn't had this flaming urge for a feeling of importance, civilization would have been impossible. Without it, we should have been just about like animals.

It was this desire for a feeling of importance that led an uneducated, poverty-stricken grocery clerk to study some law books he found in the bottom of a barrel of household plunder that he had bought for fifty cents. You have probably heard of this grocery clerk. His name was Lincoln.

It was this desire for a feeling of importance that inspired Dickens to write his immortal novels. This desire inspired Sir Christopher Wren to design his symphonies in stone. This desire made Rockefeller amass millions that he never spent! And this same desire made the richest family in your town build a house far too large for its requirements.

This desire makes you want to wear the latest styles, drive the latest cars and talk about your brilliant children.

It is this desire that lures many boys and girls into joining gangs and engaging in criminal activities. The average young criminal, according to E.P. Mulrooney, onetime police commissioner of New York, is filled with ego, and his first request after arrest is for those lurid newspapers that make him out a hero. The disagreeable prospect of serving time seems remote so long as he can gloat over his likeness sharing space with pictures of sports figures, movie and TV stars and politicians.

If you tell me how you get your feeling of importance, I'll tell you what you are. That determines your character. That is the most significant thing about you. For example, John D. Rockefeller got his feeling of importance by giving money to erect a modern hospital in Peking, China, to care for millions of poor people whom he had never seen and never would see. Dillinger, on the other hand, got his feeling of importance by being a bandit, a bank robber and killer. When the FBI agents were hunting him, he dashed into a farmhouse up in Minnesota and said, "I'm Dillinger!" He was proud of the fact that he was Public Enemy Number One. "I'm not going to hurt you, but I'm Dillinger!" he said.

Yes, the one significant difference between Dillinger and Rockefeller is how they got their feeling of importance.

History sparkles with amusing examples of famous people struggling for a feeling of importance. Even George Washington wanted to be called "His Mightiness, the President of the United States"; and Columbus pleaded for the title "Admiral of the Ocean and Viceroy of India". Catherine the Great refused to open letters that were not addressed to "Her Imperial Majesty"; and Mrs. Lincoln, in the White House, turned upon Mrs. Grant like a tigress and shouted, "How dare you be seated in my presence until I invite you!"

Our millionaires helped finance Admiral Byrd's expedition to the Antarctic in 1928 with the understanding that ranges of icy mountains would be named after them; and Victor Hugo aspired to have nothing less than the city of Paris renamed in his honor. Even Shakespeare, mightiest of the mighty, tried to add luster to his name by procuring a coat of arms for his family.

People sometimes become invalids in order to win sympathy and attention, and get a feeling of importance. For example, take Mrs. McKinley. She got a feeling of importance by forcing her husband, the President of the United States, to neglect important affairs of state while he reclined on the bed beside her for hours at a time, his arm about her, soothing her to sleep. She fed her gnawing desire for attention by insisting that he remain with her while she was having her teeth fixed, and once created a stormy scene when he had to leave her alone with the dentist while he kept an appointment with John Hay, his secretary of state.

The writer Mary Roberts Rinehart once told me of a bright, vigorous young woman who became an invalid in order to get a feeling of importance. "One day," said Mrs. Rinehart, "this woman had been obliged to face something, her age perhaps. The lonely years were stretching ahead and there was little left for her to anticipate.

"She took to her bed; and for ten years her old mother traveled to the third floor and back, carrying trays, nursing her. Then one day the old mother, weary with service, lay down and died. For some weeks, the invalid languished; then she got up, put on her clothing, and resumed living again."

Some authorities declare that people may actually go insane in order to find, in the dreamland of insanity, the feeling of importance that has been denied them in the harsh world of reality. There are more patients suffering from mental diseases in the United States than from all other diseases combined.

What is the cause of insanity?

Nobody can answer such a sweeping question, but we know that certain diseases, such as syphilis, break down and destroy the brain cells and result in insanity. In fact, about one-half of all mental diseases can be attributed to such physical causes as brain lesions, alcohol, toxins and injuries. But the other half—and this is the appalling part of the story—the other half of the people who go insane apparently have nothing organically wrong with their brain cells. In post-mortem examinations, when their brain tissues are studied under the highest-powered microscopes, these tissues are found to be apparently just as healthy as yours and mine.

Why do these people go insane?

I put that question to the head physician of one of our most important psychiatric hospitals. This doctor, who has received the highest honors and the most coveted awards for his knowledge of this subject, told me frankly that he didn't know why people went insane. Nobody knows for sure. But he did say that many people who go insane find in insanity a feeling of importance that they were unable to achieve in the world of reality. Then he told me this story:

"I have a patient right now whose marriage proved to be a tragedy. She wanted love, sexual gratification, children and social prestige, but life blasted all her hopes. Her husband didn't love her. He refused even to eat with her and forced her to serve his meals in his room upstairs. She had no children, no social standing. She went insane; and, in her imagination, she divorced her husband and resumed her maiden name. She now believes she has married into English aristocracy, and she insists on being called Lady Smith.

"And as for children, she imagines now that she has had a new child every night. Each time I call on her she says: 'Doctor, I had a baby last night.'"

Life once wrecked all her dream ships on the sharp rocks of reality; but in the sunny, fantasy isles of insanity, all her barkentines race into port with canvas billowing and winds winging through the masts.

Tragic? Oh, I don't know. Her physician said to me: "If I could stretch out my hand and restore her sanity, I wouldn't do it. She's much happier as she is."

MONETIZING YOUR TALK

If some people are so hungry for a feeling of importance that they actually go insane to get it, imagine what miracle you and I can achieve by giving people honest appreciation this side of insanity.

Sincere appreciation was one of the secrets of the first John D. Rockefeller's success in handling men. For example, when one of his partners, Edward T. Bedford, lost a million dollars for the firm by a bad buy in South America, John D. might have criticized; but he knew Bedford had done his best—and the incident was closed. So Rockefeller found something to praise; he congratulated Bedford because he had been able to save 60 per cent of the money he had invested. "That's splendid," said Rockefeller. "We don't always do as well as that upstairs."

We nourish the bodies of our children and friends and employees, but how seldom do we nourish their self-esteem? We provide them with roast beef and potatoes to build energy, but we neglect to give them kind words of appreciation that would sing in their memories for years like the music of the morning stars.

Some readers are saying right now as they read these lines: "Oh, phooey! *Flattery! Bear oil!* I've tried that stuff. It doesn't work—not with intelligent people."

Of course flattery seldom works with discerning people. It is shallow, selfish and insincere. It ought to fail and it usually does. True, some people are so hungry, so thirsty, for appreciation that they will swallow anything, just as a starving man will eat grass and fishworms.

Even Queen Victoria was susceptible to flattery. Prime Minister Benjamin Disraeli confessed that he put it on thick in dealing with the Queen. To use his exact words, he said he "spread it on with a trowel". But Disraeli was one of the most polished, deft and adroit men who ever ruled the far-flung British Empire. He was a genius in his line. What would work for him wouldn't necessarily work for you and me. In the long run, flattery will do you more harm than good. Flattery is counterfeit, and like counterfeit money, it will eventually get you into trouble if you pass it to someone else.

The difference between appreciation and flattery? That is simple. One is sincere and the other insincere. One comes from the heart out; the other from the teeth out. One is unselfish; the other selfish. One is universally admired; the other universally condemned.

IT DOESN'T COST YOU TO PRAISE

I recently saw a bust of Mexican hero General Alvaro Obregon in the Chapultepec palace in Mexico City. Below the bust are carved these wise words from General Obregon's philosophy: "Don't be afraid of enemies who attack you. Be afraid of the friends who flatter you."

No! No! No! I am not suggesting flattery! Far from it. I'm talking about a new way of life. Let me repeat. *I am talking about a new way of life.*

King George V had a set of six maxims displayed on the walls of his study at Buckingham Palace. One of these maxims said: "Teach me neither to proffer nor receive cheap praise." That's all flattery is—cheap praise. I once read a definition of flattery that may be worth repeating: "Flattery is telling the other person precisely what he thinks about himself."

"Use what language you will," said Ralph Waldo Emerson, "you can never say anything but what you are."

If all we had to do was flatter, everybody would catch on and we should all be experts in human relations.

When we are not engaged in thinking about some definite problem, we usually spend about 95 per cent of our time thinking about ourselves. Now, if we stop thinking about ourselves for a while and begin to think of the other person's good points, we won't have to resort to flattery so cheap and false that it can be spotted almost before it is out of the mouth.

One of the most neglected virtues of our daily existence is appreciation. Somehow, we neglect to praise our son or daughter when he or she brings home a good report card, and we fail to encourage our children when they first succeed in baking a cake or building a birdhouse. Nothing pleases children more than this kind of parental interest and approval.

The next time you enjoy filet mignon at the club, send word to the chef that it was excellently prepared, and when a tired salesperson shows you unusual courtesy, please mention it.

Every minister, lecturer and public speaker knows the discouragement of pouring himself or herself out to an audience and not receiving a single ripple of appreciative comment. What applies to professionals applies doubly to workers in offices, shops and factories and our families and friends. In our interpersonal relations we should never forget that all our associates are human beings and hunger for appreciation. It is the legal tender that all souls enjoy.

Try leaving a friendly trail of little sparks of gratitude on your daily trips. You will be surprised how they will set small flames of friendship that will be rose beacons on your next visit.

Honest appreciation gets results where criticism and ridicule fail.

Hurting people not only does not change them, it is never called for. There is an old saying that I have cut out and pasted on my mirror where I cannot help but see it every day:

I shall pass this way but once; any good, therefore, that I can do or any kindness that I can show to any human being, let me do it now. Let me not defer nor neglect it, for I shall not pass this way again.

Emerson said: "Every man I meet is my superior in some way. In that, I learn of him."

If that was true of Emerson, isn't it likely to be a thousand times more true of you and me? Let's cease thinking of our accomplishments, our wants. Let's try to figure out the other person's good points. Then forget flattery. Give honest, sincere appreciation. Be "hearty in your approbation and lavish in your praise" and people will cherish your words and treasure them and repeat them over a lifetime—repeat them years after you have forgotten them.

POINTS TO REMEMBER

1. The only way you can get someone to do anything is by giving them what they want.
2. The "craving" to be appreciated is universal.
3. Honest appreciation gets results where criticism and ridicule fail.

3

BECOME A GOOD CONVERSATIONALIST

What is the secret, the mystery, of a successful business interview? Well, according to former Harvard president Charles W. Eliot, "There is no mystery about successful business intercourse. Exclusive attention to the person who is speaking to you is very important. Nothing else is so flattering as that."

Eliot himself was a past master of the art of listening. Henry James, one of America's first great novelists, recalled: "Dr. Eliot's listening was not mere silence, but a form of activity. Sitting very erect on the end of his spine with hands joined in his lap, making no movement except that he revolved his thumbs around each other faster or slower, he faced his interlocutor and seemed to be hearing with his eyes as well as his ears. He listened with his mind and attentively considered what you had to say while you said it… At the end of an interview the person who had talked to him felt that he had had his say."

Self-evident, isn't it? You don't have to study for four years in Harvard to discover that. Yet I know and you know department store owners who will rent expensive space, buy their goods economically, dress their windows appealingly, spend thousands of dollars in advertising and then hire clerks who haven't the sense to be good listeners—clerks who interrupt customers, contradict them, irritate them and all but drive them from the store.

A STRONG DOSE OF SYMPATHY

Listening is just as important in one's home life as in the world of business. Millie Esposito of Croton-on- Hudson, New York, made it her business to listen carefully when one of her children wanted to speak with her. One evening she was sitting in the kitchen with her son, Robert, and after a brief discussion of something that was on his mind, Robert said: "Mom, I know that you love me very much."

Mrs. Esposito was touched and said: "Of course I love you very much. Did you doubt it?"

Robert responded: "No, but I really know you love me because whenever I want to talk to you about something you stop whatever you are doing and listen to me."

The chronic kicker, even the most violent critic, will frequently soften and be subdued in the presence of a patient, sympathetic listener—a listener who will be silent while the irate fault-finder dilates like a king cobra and spews the poison out of his system. To illustrate: The New York Telephone Company discovered a few years ago that it had to deal with one of the most vicious customers who ever cursed a customer service representative. And he did curse. He raved. He threatened to tear the phone out by its roots. He refused to pay certain charges that he declared were false. He wrote letters to the newspapers. He filed innumerable complaints with the Public Service Commission, and he started several suits against the telephone company.

At last, one of the company's most skillful "troubleshooters" was sent to interview this stormy petrel. This "troubleshooter" listened and let the cantankerous customer enjoy himself pouring out his tirade. The telephone representative listened and said "yes" and sympathized with his grievance.

"He raved on and I listened for nearly three hours," the "troubleshooter" said as he related his experiences before one of the author's classes. "Then I went back and listened some more. I interviewed him four times, and before the fourth visit was over I had become a charter member of an organization he was starting. He called it the 'Telephone Subscribers Protective Association.' I am still a member of this organization, and, so far as I know, I'm the only member in the world today besides Mr. —.

"I listened and sympathized with him on every point that he had made during these interviews. He had never had a telephone representative talk with him that way before, and he became almost friendly. The point on which I went to see him was not even mentioned on the first visit, nor was it mentioned on the second or third, but upon the fourth interview, I closed the case completely, he paid all his bills in full, and for the first time in the history of his difficulties with the telephone company he voluntarily withdrew his complaints from the Public Service Commission."

Doubtless Mr. — had considered himself a holy crusader, defending the public rights against callous exploitation. But in reality, what he had really wanted was a feeling of importance. He got this feeling of importance at first by kicking and complaining. But as soon as he got his feeling of importance from a representative of the company, his imagined grievances vanished into thin air.

One morning years ago, an angry customer stormed into the office of Julian F. Detmer, founder of the Detmer Woolen

Company, which later became the world's largest distributor of woolens to the tailoring trade.

"This man owed us a small sum of money," Mr. Detmer explained to me. "The customer denied it, but we knew he was wrong. So our credit department had insisted that he pay. After getting a number of letters from our credit department, he packed his grip, made a trip to Chicago, and hurried into my office to inform me not only that he was not going to pay that bill, but that he was never going to buy another dollar's worth of goods from the Detmer Woolen Company.

"I listened patiently to all he had to say. I was tempted to interrupt, but I realized that would be bad policy. So I let him talk himself out. When he finally simmered down and got in a receptive mood, I said quietly: 'I want to thank you for coming to Chicago to tell me about this. You have done me a great favor, for if our credit department has annoyed you, it may annoy other good customers, and that would be just too bad. Believe me, I am far more eager to hear this than you are to tell it.'

"That was the last thing in the world he expected me to say. I think he was a trifle disappointed, because he had come to Chicago to tell me a thing or two, but here I was thanking him instead of scrapping with him. I assured him we would wipe the charge off the books and forget it, because he was a very careful man with only one account to look after, while our clerks had to look after thousands. Therefore, he was less likely to be wrong than we were.

"I told him that I understood exactly how he felt and that, if I were in his shoes, I should undoubtedly feel precisely as he did. Since he wasn't going to buy from us anymore, I recommended some other woolen houses.

"In the past, we had usually lunched together when he came

to Chicago, so I invited him to have lunch with me this day. He accepted reluctantly, but when we came back to the office he placed a larger order than ever before. He returned home in a softened mood and, wanting to be just as fair with us as we had been with him, looked over his bills, found one had been mislaid, and sent us a cheque with his apologies.

"Later, when his wife presented him with a baby boy, he gave his son the middle name of Detmer, and he remained a friend and customer of the house until his death 22 years afterwards."

TECHNIQUE TO EITHER ATTRACT OR REPEL

Years ago, a poor Dutch immigrant boy washed the windows of a bakery shop after school to help support his family. His people were so poor that in addition he used to go out in the street with a basket every day and collect stray bits of coal that had fallen in the gutter where the coal wagons had delivered fuel. That boy, Edward Bok, never got more than six years of schooling in his life; yet eventually he made himself one of the most successful magazine editors in the history of American journalism. How did he do it? That is a long story, but how he got his start can be told briefly. He got his start by using the principles in this chapter.

He left school when he was 13, and became an office boy for Western Union, but he didn't for one moment give up the idea of an education. Instead, he started to educate himself. He saved his carfares and went without lunch until he had enough money to buy an encyclopedia of American biography—and then he did an unheard-of thing. He read the lives of famous people and wrote to them asking for additional information about their childhoods. He was a good listener. He asked famous people to tell him more about themselves. He wrote to General James A. Garfield, who was then running for President, and asked if it was true that he was once a tow boy on a canal; and Garfield replied. He wrote to General Grant asking about a certain battle, and Grant drew a map for him and invited this 14-year-old boy to dinner and spent the evening talking to him.

Soon our Western Union messenger boy was corresponding with many of the most famous people in the nation: Ralph Waldo Emerson, Oliver Wendell Holmes, Longfellow, Mrs. Abraham Lincoln, Louisa May Alcott, General Sherman and Jefferson Davis. Not only did he correspond with these distinguished people, but as soon as he got a vacation, he visited many of them as a welcome guest in their homes. This experience imbued him with a confidence that was invaluable. These men and women fired him with a vision and ambition that shaped his life. And all this, let me repeat, was made possible solely by the application of the principles we are discussing here.

Isaac F. Marcosson, a journalist who interviewed hundreds of celebrities, declared that many people fail to make a favorable impression because they don't listen attentively. "They have been so much concerned with what they are going to say next that they do not keep their ears open… Very important people have told me that they prefer good listeners to good talkers, but the ability to listen seems rarer than almost any other good trait."

And not only important personages crave a good listener, but ordinary folk do too. As the *Reader's Digest* once said: "Many persons call a doctor when all they want is an audience."

During the darkest hours of the Civil War, Lincoln wrote to an old friend in Springfield, Illinois, asking him to come to Washington. Lincoln said he had some problems he wanted to discuss with him. The old neighbor called at the White House, and Lincoln talked to him for hours about the advisability of issuing a proclamation freeing the slaves. Lincoln went over all the arguments for and against such a move, and then read letters and newspaper articles, some denouncing him for not freeing the slaves and others denouncing him for fear he was going to free them. After talking for hours, Lincoln shook hands with his old neighbor, said good night, and sent him back to Illinois without even asking for his opinion. Lincoln had done all the talking himself. That seemed to clarify his mind. "He seemed to feel easier after that talk," the old friend said. Lincoln hadn't wanted advice. He had wanted merely a friendly, sympathetic listener to whom he could unburden himself. That's what we all want when we are in trouble. That is frequently all the irritated customer wants, and the dissatisfied employee or the hurt friend.

One of the great listeners of modern times was Sigmund Freud. A man who met Freud described his manner of listening. "It struck me so forcibly that I shall never forget him. He had qualities which I had never seen in any other man. Never had I seen such concentrated attention. There was none of the piercing 'soul penetrating gaze' business. His eyes were mild and genial. His voice was low and kind. His gestures were few. But the attention he gave me, his appreciation of what I said, even when I said it badly, was extraordinary. *You've no idea what it meant to be listened to like that.*"

If you want to know how to make people shun you and laugh at you behind your back and even despise you, here is the recipe: Never listen to anyone for long. Talk incessantly about yourself. If you have an idea while the other person is talking, don't wait for him or her to finish: bust right in and interrupt in the middle of a sentence.

Do you know people like that? I do, unfortunately; and

the astonishing part of it is that some of them are prominent.

Bores, that is all they are—bores intoxicated with their own egos, drunk with a sense of their own importance.

People who talk only of themselves think only of themselves. And "those people who think only of themselves," Dr. Nicholas Murray Butler, longtime president of Columbia University, said, "are hopelessly uneducated. They are not educated, no matter how instructed they may be." So if you aspire to be a good conversationalist, be an attentive listener. To be interesting, be interested. Ask questions that other persons will enjoy answering. Encourage them to talk about themselves and their accomplishments.

Remember that the people you are talking to are a hundred times more interested in themselves and their wants and problems than they are in you and your problems. A person's toothache means more to that person than a famine in China which kills a million people. A boil on one's neck interests one more than 40 earthquakes in Africa. Think of that the next time you start a conversation.

POINTS TO REMEMBER

1. A good conversationalist is a good listener first.
2. Being attentive is appreciated.
3. Encourage others to have a conversation with you by appearing interested.

4

UNDERSTAND THE OTHER'S POINT OF VIEW

I often went fishing up in Maine during the summer. Personally I am very fond of strawberries and cream, but I have found that for some strange reason, fish prefer worms. So when I went fishing, I didn't think about what I wanted. I didn't bait the hook with strawberries and cream. Rather, I dangled a worm or a grasshopper in front of the fish and said: "Wouldn't you like to have that?"

Why not use the same common sense when fishing for people?

That is what Lloyd George, Great Britain's Prime Minister during World War I, did. When someone asked him how he managed to stay in power after the other wartime leaders— Wilson, Orlando and Clemenceau—had been forgotten, he replied that if his staying on top might be attributed to any one thing, it would be to his having learned that it was necessary to bait the hook to suit the fish.

Why talk about what we want? That is childish. Absurd. Of course, you are interested in what you want. You are eternally interested in it. But no one else is. The rest of us are just like you: we are interested in what we want.

So the only way on earth to influence other people is to talk about what *they* want and show them how to get it.

Remember that tomorrow when you are trying to get somebody to do something. If, for example, you don't want your children to smoke, don't preach at them, and don't talk about what you want; but show them that cigarettes may keep them from making the basketball team or winning the hundred-yard dash.

Every act you have ever performed since the day you were born was performed because you wanted something. How about the time you gave a large contribution to the Red Cross? Yes, that is no exception to the rule. You gave the Red Cross the donation because you wanted to lend a helping hand; you wanted to do a beautiful, unselfish, divine act. "In as much as ye have done it unto one of the least of these my brethren, ye have done it unto me."

If you hadn't wanted that feeling more than you wanted your money, you would not have made the contribution. Of course, you might have made the contribution because you were ashamed to refuse or because a customer asked you to do it. But one thing is certain. You made the contribution because you wanted something.

POINTS TO REMEMBER

1. The only way to influence people is by talking about what they want.
2. No charitable act is ever selfless.
3. Personal interest is always preferred over collective interest.

5

LET THE OTHER PERSON SAVE FACE

Years ago the General Electric Company was faced with the delicate task of removing Charles Steinmetz from the head of a department. Steinmetz, a genius of the first magnitude when it came to electricity, was a failure as the head of the calculating department. Yet the company didn't dare offend the man. He was indispensable—and highly sensitive. So they gave him a new title. They made him Consulting Engineer of the General Electric Company—a new title for work he was already doing—and let someone else head up the department.

Steinmetz was happy.

So were the officers of G.E. They had gently maneuvered their most temperamental star, and they had done it without a storm—by letting him save face.

AN ACT OF KINDNESS

Letting one save face! How important, how vitally important that is! And how few of us ever stop to think of it! We ride roughshod over the feelings of others, getting our own way, finding fault, issuing threats, criticizing a child or an employee in front of others, without even considering the hurt to the other person's pride. Whereas a few minutes' thought, a considerate word or two, a genuine understanding of the other person's attitude, would go so far toward alleviating the sting!

Let's remember that the next time we are faced with the distasteful necessity of discharging or reprimanding an employee.

"Firing employees is not much fun. Getting fired is even less fun." (I'm quoting now from a letter written me by Marshall A. Granger, a certified public accountant.) "Our business is mostly seasonal. Therefore we have to let a lot of people go after the income tax rush is over.

"It's a byword in our profession that no one enjoys wielding the axe. Consequently, the custom has developed of getting it over as soon as possible, and usually in the following way: 'Sit down, Mr. Smith. The season's over, and we don't seem to see any more assignments for you. Of course, you understood you were only employed for the busy season anyhow, etc., etc.'

"The effect on these people is one of disappointment and a feeling of being 'let down'. Most of them are in the accounting field for life, and they retain no particular love for the firm that drops them so casually.

"I recently decided to let our seasonal personnel go with a little more tact and consideration. So I call each one in only after carefully thinking over his or her work during the winter. And I've said something like this: 'Mr. Smith, you've done a fine job (if he has). That time we sent you to Newark, you had a tough assignment. You were on the spot, but you came through with flying colors, and we want you to know the firm is proud of you. You've got the stuff—you're going a long way, wherever you're working. This firm believes in you, and is rooting for you, and we don't want you to forget it.'

"Effect? The people go away feeling a lot better about being fired. They don't feel 'let down'. They know if we had work for them, we'd keep them on. And when we need them again, they come to us with a keen personal affection."

At one session of our course, two class members discussed the negative effects of faultfinding versus the positive effects of letting the other person save face.

Fred Clark of Harrisburg, Pennsylvania, told of an incident that occurred in his company: "At one of our production meetings, a vice president was asking very pointed questions of one of our production supervisors regarding a production process. His tone of voice was aggressive and aimed at pointing out faulty performance on the part of the supervisor. Not wanting to be embarrassed in front of his peers, the supervisor was evasive in his responses. This caused the vice president to lose his temper, berate the supervisor and accuse him of lying.

"Any working relationship that might have existed prior to this encounter was destroyed in a few brief moments. This supervisor, who was basically a good worker, was useless to our company from that time on. A few months later he left our firm and went to work for a competitor, where I understand he is doing a fine job."

Another class member, Anna Mazzone, related how a similar incident had occurred at her job—but what a difference in approach and results! Ms. Mazzone, a marketing specialist for a food packer, was given her first major assignment—the test-marketing of a new product. She told the class: "When the results of the test came in, I was devastated. I had made a serious error in my planning, and the entire test had to be done all over again. To make this worse, I had no time to discuss it with my boss before the meeting in which I was to make my report on the project.

"When I was called on to give the report, I was shaking with fright. I had all I could do to keep from breaking down, but I resolved I would not cry and have all those men make remarks about women not being able to handle a management job because they are too emotional. I made my report briefly and stated that due to an error I would repeat the study before the next meeting. I sat down, expecting my boss to blow up.

"Instead, he thanked me for my work and remarked that it was not unusual for a person to make an error on a new project and that he had confidence that the repeat survey would be accurate and meaningful to the company. He assured me, in front of all my colleagues, that he had faith in me and knew I had done my best, and that my lack of experience, not my lack of ability, was the reason for the failure.

"I left that meeting with my head up in the air and with the determination that I would never let that boss of mine down again."

Even if we are right and the other person is definitely wrong, we only destroy ego by causing someone to lose face. The legendary French aviation pioneer and author Antoine de Saint-Exupéry wrote: "I have no right to say or do anything that diminishes a man in his own eyes. What matters is not what I think of him, but what he thinks of himself. Hurting a man in his dignity is a crime."

A real leader will always follow...

POINTS TO REMEMBER

1. It's better for you to not hurt someone's pride.
2. Be a conscientious leader.
3. Kindness doesn't cost you anything.

6

INFLUENCING BY SUGGESTION

When we weigh, compare, and decide upon the value of any given ideas, we reason; when an idea produces in us an opinion or an action, without first being subjected to deliberation, we are moved by suggestion.

Man was formerly thought to be a reasoning animal, basing his actions on the conclusions of natural logic. It was supposed that before forming an opinion or deciding on a course of conduct he weighed at least some of the reasons for and against the matter, and performed a more or less simple process of reasoning. But modern research has shown that quite the opposite is true. Most of our opinions and actions are not based upon conscious reasoning, but are the result of suggestion. In fact, some authorities declare that an act of pure reasoning is very rare in the average mind. Momentous decisions are made, far-reaching actions are determined upon, primarily by the force of suggestion.

Notice that word "primarily," for simple thought, and even mature reasoning, often follows a suggestion accepted in the mind, and the thinker fondly supposes that his conclusion is from first to last based on cold logic.

THE BASIS OF SUGGESTION

We must think of suggestion both as an effect and as a cause. Considered as an effect, or objectively, there must be something in the hearer that predisposes him to receive suggestion; considered as a cause, or subjectively, there must be some methods by which the speaker can move upon that particularly susceptible attitude of the hearer. How to do this honestly and fairly is our problem—to do it dishonestly and trickily, to use suggestion to bring about conviction and action without a basis of right and truth and in a bad cause, is to assume the terrible responsibility that must fall on the champion of error. Jesus scorned not to use suggestion so that he might move men to their benefit, but every vicious trickster has adopted the same means to reach base ends. Therefore honest men will examine well into their motives and into the truth of their cause, before seeking to influence men by suggestion.

Three fundamental conditions make us all susceptive to suggestion:

We naturally respect authority. In every mind this is only a question of degree, ranging from the subject who is easily hypnotized to the stubborn mind that fortifies itself the more strongly with every assault upon its opinion. The latter type is almost immune to suggestion.

One of the singular things about suggestion is that it is rarely a fixed quantity. The mind that is receptive to the authority of a certain person may prove inflexible to another; moods and environments that produce hypnosis readily in one instance may be entirely inoperative in another; and some minds can scarcely ever be thus moved. We do know, however, that the feeling of the subject authority—influence, power, domination, control, whatever you wish to call it—lies in the person of the suggester, is the basis of all suggestion.

The extreme force of this influence is demonstrated in hypnotism. The hypnotic subject is told that he is in the water; he accepts the statement as true and makes swimming motions. He is told that a band is marching down the street, playing The Star Spangled Banner; he declares he hears the music, arises and stands with head bared.

In the same way some speakers are able to achieve a modified hypnotic effect upon their audiences. The hearers will applaud measures and ideas which, after individual reflection, they will repudiate unless such reflection brings the conviction that the first impression is correct.

A second important principle is that our feelings, thoughts and wills tend to follow the line of least resistance. Once open the mind to the sway of one feeling and it requires a greater power of feeling, thought, or will—or even all three—to unseat it. Our feelings influence our judgments and volitions much more than we care to admit. So true is this that it is a superhuman task to get an audience to reason fairly on a subject on which it feels deeply, and when this result is accomplished the success becomes noteworthy, as in the case of Henry Ward Beecher's Liverpool speech. Emotional ideas once accepted are soon cherished, and finally become our very inmost selves. Attitudes based on feelings alone are prejudices.

What is true of our feelings, in this respect, applies to our ideas: All thoughts that enter the mind tend to be accepted as truth unless a stronger and contradictory thought arises.

The speaker skilled in moving men to action manages to dominate the minds of his audience with his thoughts by subtly prohibiting the entertaining of ideas hostile to his own. Most of us are captured by the latest strong attack, and if we can be induced to act while under the stress of that last insistent thought, we lose sight of counter influences. The fact is that almost all our decisions—if they involve thought at all—are of this sort: at the moment of decision the course of action then under contemplation usurps the attention, and conflicting ideas are dropped out of consideration.

The head of a large publishing house remarked only recently that 90 per cent of the people who bought books by subscription never read them. They buy because the salesman presents his wares so skillfully that every consideration but the attractiveness of the book drops out of the mind, and that thought prompts action. Every idea that enters the mind will result in action unless a contradictory thought arises to prohibit it. Think of singing the musical scale and it will result in your singing it unless the counter-thought of its futility or absurdity inhibits your action. If you bandage and "doctor" a horse's foot, he will go lame. You cannot think of swallowing, without the muscles used in that process being affected. You cannot think of saying "hello," without a slight movement of the muscles of speech. To warn children that they should not put beans up their noses is the surest method of getting them to do it. Every thought called up in the mind of your audience will work either for or against you. Thoughts are not dead matter; they radiate dynamic energy—the thoughts all tend to pass into action. "Thought is another name for fate." Dominate your hearers' thoughts, allay all contradictory ideas, and you will sway them as you wish.

Volitions as well as feelings and thoughts tend to follow the line of least resistance. That is what makes habit. Suggest to a man that it is impossible to change his mind and in most cases it becomes more difficult to do so—the exception is the man who naturally jumps to the contrary. Counter suggestion is the only way to reach him. Suggest subtly and persistently that the opinions of those in the audience who are opposed to your views are changing, and it requires an effort of the will—in fact, a summoning of the forces of feeling, thought and will—to stem the tide of change that has subconsciously set in.

But, not only are we moved by authority, and tend toward channels of least resistance: we are all influenced by our environments. It is difficult to rise above the sway of a crowd—its enthusiasms and its fears are contagious because they are suggestive. What so many feel, we say to ourselves, must have some basis in truth. Ten times ten makes more than one hundred. Set ten men to speaking to ten audiences of ten men each, and compare the aggregate power of those ten speakers with that of one man addressing one hundred men. The ten speakers may be more logically convincing than the single orator, but the chances are strongly in favor of the one man's reaching a greater total effect, for the hundred men will radiate conviction and resolution as ten small groups could not. We all know the truism about the enthusiasm of numbers.

Environment controls us unless the contrary is strongly suggested. A gloomy day, in a drab room, sparsely tenanted by listeners, invites platform disaster. Everyone feels it in the air. But let the speaker walk squarely up to the issue and suggest by all his feeling, manner and words that this is going to be a great gathering in every vital sense, and see how the suggestive power of environment recedes before the advance of a more potent suggestion—if such the speaker is able to make it.

Now these three factors—respect for authority, tendency to follow lines of least resistance, and susceptibility to environment—all help to bring the auditor into a state of mind favorable to suggestive influences, but they also react on the speaker, and now we must consider those personally causative, or subjective, forces which enable him to use suggestion effectively.

HOW THE SPEAKER CAN MAKE SUGGESTION EFFECTIVE

We have seen that under the influence of authoritative suggestion the audience is inclined to accept the speaker's assertion without argument and criticism. But the audience is not in this state of mind unless it has implicit confidence in the speaker. If they lack faith in him, question his motives or knowledge, or even object to his manner they will not be moved by his most logical conclusion and will fail to give him a just hearing. It is all a matter of their confidence in him. Whether the speaker finds it already in the warm, expectant look of his hearers, or must win to it against opposition or coldness, he must gain that one great vantage point before his suggestions take on power in the hearts of his listeners. Confidence is the mother of Conviction.

To secure confidence, be confident. How can you expect others to accept a message in which you lack, or seem to lack, faith yourself? Confidence is as contagious as disease. Napoleon rebuked an officer for using the word "impossible" in his presence. The speaker who will entertain no idea of defeat begets in his hearers the idea of his victory. Lady Macbeth was so confident of success that Macbeth changed his mind about undertaking the assassination. Columbus was so certain in his mission that Queen Isabella pawned her jewels to finance his expedition. Assert your message with implicit assurance, and your own belief will act as so much gunpowder to drive it home.

Advertisers have long utilized this principle. "The machine you will eventually buy," "Ask the man who owns one," "Has the strength of Gibraltar," are publicity slogans so full of confidence that they give birth to confidence in the mind of the reader.

It should—but may not!—go without saying that confidence

must have a solid ground of merit or there will be a ridiculous crash. It is all very well for the "spellbinder" to claim all the precincts—the official count is just ahead. The reaction against over-confidence and over-suggestion ought to warn those whose chief asset is mere bluff.

BE THE FACE OF CREDIBILITY

Authority is a factor in suggestion. We generally accept as truth, and without criticism, the words of an authority. When he speaks, contradictory ideas rarely arise in the mind to inhibit the action he suggests. A judge of the Supreme Court has the power of his words multiplied by the virtue of his position. The ideas of the U.S. Commissioner of Immigration on his subject are much more effective and powerful than those of a soap manufacturer, though the latter may be an able economist.

This principle also has been used in advertising. We are told that the physicians to two Kings have recommended Sanatogen. We are informed that the largest bank in America, Tiffany and Co., and The State, War, and Navy Departments, all use the Encyclopedia Britannica. The shrewd promoter gives stock in his company to influential bankers or business men in the community in order that he may use their examples as a selling argument.

If you wish to influence your audience through suggestion, if you would have your statements accepted without criticism or argument, you should appear in the light of an authority—and be one. Ignorance and credulity will remain unchanged unless the suggestion of authority be followed promptly by facts. Don't claim authority unless you carry your license in your pocket. Let reason support the position that suggestion has assumed.

Advertising will help to establish your reputation—it is "up to you" to maintain it. One speaker found that his reputation as a magazine writer was a splendid asset as a speaker. Mr. Bryan's publicity, gained by three nominations for the presidency and his position as Secretary of State, helps him to command large sums as a speaker. But—back of it all, he is a great speaker. Newspaper announcements, all kinds of advertising, formality, impressive introductions, all have a capital effect on the attitude of the audience. But how ridiculous are all these if a toy pistol is advertised as a sixteen-inch gun!

Authority is the great weapon against doubt, but even its force can rarely prevail against prejudice and persistent wrong-headedness. If any speaker has been able to forge a sword that is warranted to piece such armor, let him bless humanity by sharing his secret with his platform brethren everywhere, for thus far he is alone in his glory.

There is a middle-ground between the suggestion of authority and the confession of weakness that offers a wide range for tact in the speaker. No one can advise you when to throw your "hat in the ring" and say defiantly at the outstart, "Gentlemen, I am here to fight!" Theodore Roosevelt can do that—Beecher would have been mobbed if he had begun in that style at Liverpool. It is for your own tact to decide whether you will use the disarming grace of Henry W. Grady's introduction just quoted (even the time-worn joke was ingenuous and seemed to say, "Gentlemen, I come to you with no carefully-palmed coins"), or whether the solemn gravity of Mr. Bryan before the Convention will prove to be more effective. Only be sure that your opening attitude is well thought out, and if it change as you warm up to your subject, let not the change lay you open to a revulsion of feeling in your audience.

Example is a powerful means of suggestion. As we saw while thinking of environment in its effects on an audience, we do, without the usual amount of hesitation and criticism, what others are doing. Paris wears certain hats and gowns; the rest of the world imitates. The child mimics the actions, accents and intonations of the parent. Were a child never to hear anyone speak, he would never acquire the power of speech, unless under most arduous training, and even then only imperfectly. One of the biggest department stores in the United States spends fortunes on one advertising slogan: "Everybody is going to the big store." That makes everybody want to go.

You can reinforce the power of your message by showing that it has been widely accepted. Political organizations subsidize applause to create the impression that their speakers' ideas are warmly received and approved by the audience. The advocates of the commission-form of government of cities, the champions of votes for women, reserve as their strongest arguments the fact that a number of cities and states have already successfully accepted their plans. Advertisements use the testimonial for its power of suggestion.

A speech should be built on sound logical foundations, and no man should dare to speak on behalf of a fallacy. Arguing a subject, however, will necessarily arouse contradictory ideas in the mind of your audience. When immediate action or persuasion is desired, suggestion is more efficacious than argument—when both are judiciously mixed, the effect is irresistible.

POINTS TO REMEMBER

1. Most of our opinions are not based upon conscious reasoning, but are the result of suggestion.
2. The honest and fair way of influencing by suggestion.
3. Example is a powerful means of suggestion.

7

THE HIGH ROAD TO REASON

If a man's heart is rankling with discord and ill feeling toward you, you can't win him to your way of thinking with all the logic in Christendom. Scolding parents and domineering bosses and husbands and nagging wives ought to realize that people don't want to change their minds. They can't be forced or driven to agree with you or me. But they may possibly be led to, if we are gentle and friendly, ever so gentle and ever so friendly.

Lincoln said that, in effect, over a hundred years ago. Here are his words:

> It is an old and true maxim that "a drop of honey catches more flies than a gallon of gall." So with men, if you would win a man to your cause, first convince him that you are his sincere friend. Therein is a drop of honey that catches his heart; which, say what you will, is the great high road to his reason.

Business executives have learned that it pays to be friendly to strikers. For example, when twenty-five hundred employees in the White Motor Company's plant struck for higher wages and a union shop, Robert F. Black, then president of the company, didn't lose his temper and condemn and threaten and talk of tyranny and communists. He actually praised the strikers. He published an advertisement in the Cleveland papers, complimenting them on "the peaceful way in which they laid down their tools." Finding the strike pickets idle, he bought them a couple of dozen baseball bats and gloves and invited them to play ball on vacant lots. For those who preferred bowling, he rented a bowling alley.

This friendliness on Mr. Black's part did what friendliness always does: it begot friendliness. So the strikers borrowed brooms, shovels, and rubbish carts, and began picking up matches, papers, cigarette stubs, and cigar butts around the factory. Imagine it! Imagine strikers tidying up the factory grounds while battling for higher wages and recognition of the union. Such an event had never been heard of before in the long, tempestuous history of American labor wars. That strike ended with a compromise settlement within a week—ended without any ill feeling or rancor.

Daniel Webster, who looked like a god and talked like Jehovah, was one of the most successful advocates who ever pleaded a case; yet he ushered in his most powerful arguments with such friendly remarks as: "It will be for the jury to consider," "This may, perhaps, be worth thinking of," "Here are some facts that I trust you will not lose sight of," or "You, with your knowledge of human nature, will easily see the significance of these facts." No bulldozing. No high-pressure methods. No attempt to force his opinions on others. Webster used the soft-spoken, quiet, friendly approach, and it helped to make him famous.

You may never be called upon to settle a strike or address a jury, but you may want to get your rent reduced. Will the friendly approach help you then? Let's see.

O. L. Straub, an engineer, wanted to get his rent reduced. And he knew his landlord was hard-boiled. "I wrote him,"

Mr. Straub said in a speech before the class, "notifying him that I was vacating my apartment as soon as my lease expired. The truth was, I didn't want to move. I wanted to stay if I could get my rent reduced. But the situation seemed hopeless. Other tenants had tried—and failed. Everyone told me that the landlord was extremely difficult to deal with. But I said to myself, 'I am studying a course in how to deal with people, so I'll try it on him—and see how it works.'

"He and his secretary came to see me as soon as he got my letter. I met him at the door with a friendly greeting. I fairly bubbled with good will and enthusiasm. I didn't begin talking about how high the rent was. I began talking about how much I liked his apartment house. Believe me, I was 'hearty in my approbation and lavish in my praise.' I complimented him on the way he ran the building and told him I should like so much to stay for another year but I couldn't afford it.

"He had evidently never had such a reception from a tenant. He hardly knew what to make of it.

"Then he started to tell me his troubles. Complaining tenants. One had written him fourteen letters, some of them positively insulting. Another threatened to break his lease unless the landlord kept the man on the floor above from snoring. 'What a relief it is,' he said, 'to have a satisfied tenant like you.' And then, without my even asking him to do it, he offered to reduce my rent a little. I wanted more, so I named the figure I could afford to pay, and he accepted without a word.

"As he was leaving, he turned to me and asked, 'What decorating can I do for you?'

"If I had tried to get the rent reduced by the methods the other tenants were using, I am positive I should have met the same failure they encountered. It was the friendly, sympathetic, appreciative approach that won."

Dean Woodcock of Pittsburgh, Pennsylvania, is the superintendent of a department of the local electric company. His staff was called upon to repair some equipment on top of a pole. This type of work had formerly been performed by a different department and had only recently been transferred to Woodcock's section. Although his people had been trained in the work, this was the first time they had ever actually been called upon to do it. Everybody in the organization was interested in seeing if and how they could handle it. Mr. Woodcock, several of his subordinate managers, and members of other departments of the utility went to see the operation. Many cars and trucks were there, and a number of people were standing around watching the two lone men on top of the pole.

Glancing around, Woodcock noticed a man up the street getting out of his car with a camera. He began taking pictures of the scene. Utility people are extremely conscious of public relations, and suddenly Woodcock realized what this setup looked like to the man with the camera—overkill, dozens of people being called out to do a two-person job. He strolled up the street to the photographer.

"I see you're interested in our operation."

"Yes, and my mother will be more than interested. She owns stock in your company. This will be an eye-opener for her. She may even decide her investment was unwise. I've been telling her for years there's a lot of waste motion in companies like yours. This proves it. The newspapers might like these pictures, too."

"It does look like it, doesn't it? I'd think the same thing in your position. But this is a unique situation, ..." and Dean Woodcock went on to explain how this was the first job of this type for his department and how everyone from executives down was interested. He assured the man that under normal conditions two people could handle the job. The photographer put away his camera, shook Woodcock's hand, and thanked him for taking the time to explain the situation to him.

Dean Woodcock's friendly approach saved his company much embarrassment and bad publicity.

Aesop was a Greek slave who lived at the court of Croesus and spun immortal fables six hundred years before Christ. Yet the truths he taught about human nature are just as true in Boston and Birmingham now as they were twenty-six centuries ago in Athens. The sun can make you take off your coat more quickly than the wind; and kindliness, the friendly approach, and appreciation can make people change their minds more readily than all the bluster and storming in the world.

Remember what Lincoln said: "A drop of honey catches more flies than a gallon of gall."

POINTS TO REMEMBER

1. A drop of honey catches more flies than a gallon of gall.
2. A friendly and appreciative approach always works in your favor.
3. Complaining about something won't help you get it.

8

DO THIS AND YOU'LL BE WELCOME
ANYWHERE

Why read this book to find out how to win friends? Why not study the technique of the greatest winner of friends the world has ever known? Who is he? You may meet him tomorrow coming down the street. When you get within ten feet of him, he will begin to wag his tail. If you stop and pat him, he will almost jump out of his skin to show you how much he likes you. And you know that behind this show of affection on his part, there are no ulterior motives: he doesn't want to sell you any real estate, and he doesn't want to marry you.

Did you ever stop to think that a dog is the only animal that doesn't have to work for a living? A hen has to lay eggs, a cow has to give milk, and a canary has to sing. But a dog makes his living by giving you nothing but love.

When I was five years old, my father bought a little yellow-haired pup for fifty cents. He was the light and joy of my childhood. Every afternoon about four-thirty, he would sit in the front yard with his beautiful eyes staring steadfastly at the path, and as soon as he heard my voice or saw me swinging my dinner pail through the buck brush, he was off like a shot, racing breathlessly up the hill to greet me with leaps of joy and barks of sheer ecstasy.

Tippy was my constant companion for five years. Then one tragic night—I shall never forget it—he was killed within ten feet of me, killed by lightning. Tippy's death was the tragedy of my boyhood.

You never read a book on psychology, Tippy. You didn't need to. You knew by some divine instinct that you can make more friends in two months by becoming genuinely interested in other people than you can in two years by trying to get other people interested in you. Let me repeat that. You can make more friends in two months by becoming interested in other people than you can in two years by trying to get other people interested in you.

Yet I know and you know people who blunder through life trying to wigwag other people into becoming interested in them.

Of course, it doesn't work. People are not interested in you. They are not interested in me. They are interested in themselves—morning, noon, and after dinner.

The New York Telephone Company made a detailed study of telephone conversations to find out which word is the most frequently used. You have guessed it: it is the personal pronoun "I." "I." "I." It was used 3,900 times in 500 telephone conversations. "I." "I." "I." "I."

When you see a group photograph that you are in, whose picture do you look for first?

If we merely try to impress people and get people interested in us, we will never have many true, sincere friends. Friends, real friends, are not made that way.

Napoleon tried it, and in his last meeting with Josephine he said: "Josephine, I have been as fortunate as any man ever was on this earth; and yet, at this hour, you are the only person in the world on whom I can rely." And historians doubt that he could rely even on her.

I once took a course in short-story writing at New York University, and during that course the editor of a leading magazine talked to our class. He said he could pick up any one of the dozens of stories that drifted across his desk every day and after reading a few paragraphs he could feel whether or not the author liked people. "If the author doesn't like people," he said, "people won't like his or her stories."

This hard-boiled editor stopped twice in the course of his talk on fiction writing and apologized for preaching a sermon. "I am telling you," he said, "the same things your preacher would tell you, but remember, you have to be interested in people if you want to be a successful writer of stories."

If that is true of writing fiction, you can be sure it is true of dealing with people face-to-face.

I have discovered from personal experience that one can win the attention and time and cooperation of even the most sought-after people by becoming genuinely interested in them.

INVEST YOUR TIME AND ENERGY ON OTHERS

All of us, be we workers in a factory, clerks in an office, or even a king upon his throne—all of us like people who admire us. Take the German kaiser, for example. At the close of World War I, he was probably the most savagely and universally despised man on this earth. Even his own nation turned against him when he fled over into Holland to save his neck. The hatred against him was so intense that millions of people would have loved to tear him limb from limb or burn him at the stake. In the midst of all this forest fire of fury, one little boy wrote the kaiser a simple, sincere letter glowing with kindliness and admiration. This little boy said that no matter what the others thought, he would always love Wilhelm as his emperor. The kaiser was deeply touched by his letter and invited the little boy to come see him. The boy came, so did his mother—and the kaiser married her. That little boy didn't need to read a book on how to win friends and influence people. He knew how instinctively.

If we want to make friends, let's put ourselves out to do things for other people—things that require time, energy, unselfishness, and thoughtfulness. When the Duke of Windsor was Prince of Wales, he was scheduled to tour South America, and before he started out on that tour he spent months studying Spanish so that he could make public talks in the language of the country; and the South Americans loved him for it.

For years I made it a point to find out the birthdays of my friends. How? Although I haven't the foggiest bit of faith in astrology, I began by asking the other party whether he believed the date of one's birth has anything to do with character and disposition. I then asked him or her to tell me the month and day of birth. If he or she said November 24, for example, I kept repeating to myself, "November 24, November 24." The minute my friend's back was turned, I wrote down the name and birthday and later would transfer it to a birthday book. At the beginning of each year, I had these birthday dates scheduled in my calendar pad so that they came to my attention automatically. When the natal day arrived, there was my letter or telegram. What a hit it made! I was frequently the only person on earth who remembered.

If we want to make friends, let's greet people with animation and enthusiasm. When somebody calls you on the telephone use the same psychology. Say "Hello" in tones that bespeak how pleased you are to have the person call. Many companies train their telephone operators to greet all callers in a tone that radiates interest and enthusiasm. The callers feel the company is concerned about them. Let's remember that when we answer the telephone tomorrow.

Showing a genuine interest in others not only wins friends for you, but may develop in its customers a loyalty to your company

---

POINTS TO REMEMBER

1. The universal rule of "I."
2. One can win the attention and time and cooperation of even the most sought-after people by becoming genuinely interested in them.
3. Significance of relationships in personal and professional world.

9

THINK BEFORE YOU CRITICIZE

You will find examples of the futility of criticism bristling on a thousand pages of history. Take, for example, the famous quarrel between Theodore Roosevelt and President Taft—a quarrel that split the Republican party, put Woodrow Wilson in the White House and wrote bold, luminous lines across the First World War and altered the flow of history. Let's review the facts quickly. When Theodore Roosevelt stepped out of the White House in 1908, he supported Taft, who was elected President. Then Theodore Roosevelt went off to Africa to shoot lions. When he returned, he exploded. He denounced Taft for his conservatism, tried to secure the nomination for a third term himself, formed the Bull Moose party and all but demolished the G.O.P. In the election that followed, William Howard Taft and the Republican party carried only two states—Vermont and Utah. The most disastrous defeat the party had ever known.

Theodore Roosevelt blamed Taft, but did President Taft blame himself? Of course not. With tears in his eyes, Taft said: "I don't see how I could have done any differently from what I have."

Who was to blame? Roosevelt or Taft? Frankly, I don't know, and I don't care. The point I am trying to make is that all of Theodore Roosevelt's criticism didn't persuade Taft that he was wrong. It merely made Taft strive to justify himself and to reiterate with tears in his eyes: "I don't see how I could have done any differently from what I have."

Or, take the Teapot Dome oil scandal. It kept the newspapers ringing with indignation in the early 1920s. It rocked the nation! Within the memory of living men, nothing like it had ever happened before in American public life. Here are the bare facts of the scandal: Albert B. Fall, secretary of the interior in Harding's cabinet, was entrusted with the leasing of government oil reserves at Elk Hill and Teapot Dome—oil reserves that had been set aside for the future use of the Navy. Did Secretary Fall permit competitive bidding? No sir. He handed the fat, juicy contract outright to his friend Edward L. Doheny. And what did Doheny do? He gave Secretary Fall what he was pleased to call a "loan" of $100,000. Then, in a high-handed manner, Secretary Fall ordered United States Marines into the district to drive off competitors whose adjacent wells were sapping oil out of the Elk Hill reserves. These competitors, driven off their ground at the ends of guns and bayonets, rushed into court—and blew the lid off the Teapot Dome scandal. A stench arose so vile that it ruined the Harding Administration, nauseated an entire nation, threatened to wreck the Republican party and put Albert B. Fall behind prison bars.

Fall was condemned viciously—condemned as few men in public life have ever been. Did he repent? Never! Years later Herbert Hoover intimated in a public speech that President Harding's death had been due to mental anxiety and worry because a friend had betrayed him. When Mrs. Fall heard that, she sprang from her chair, she wept, she shook her fists at fate and screamed: "What! Harding betrayed by Fall? No! My husband never betrayed anyone. This whole house full of gold would not tempt my husband to do wrong. He is the one who has been betrayed and led to the slaughter and crucified."

There you are; human nature in action, wrongdoers, blaming everybody but themselves. We are all like that. So when you and I are tempted to criticize someone tomorrow, let's remember Al Capone, "Two Gun" Crowley and Albert Fall. Let's realize that criticisms are like homing pigeons. They always return home. Let's realize that the person we are going to correct and condemn will probably justify himself or herself, and condemn us in return; or, like the gentle Taft, will say: "I don't see how I could have done any differently from what I have."

On the morning of 15 April 1865, Abraham Lincoln lay dying in a hall bedroom of a cheap lodging house directly across the street from Ford's Theatre, where John Wilkes Booth had shot him. Lincoln's long body lay stretched diagonally across a sagging bed that was too short for him. A cheap reproduction of Rosa Bonheur's famous painting *The Horse Fair* hung above the bed, and a dismal gas jet flickered yellow light.

As Lincoln lay dying, Secretary of War Stanton said, "There lies the most perfect ruler of men that the world has ever seen."

What was the secret of Lincoln's success in dealing with people? I studied the life of Abraham Lincoln for ten years and devoted all of three years to writing and rewriting a book entitled *Lincoln the Unknown*. I believe I have made as detailed and exhaustive study of Lincoln's personality and home life as it is possible for any being to make. I made a special study of Lincoln's method of dealing with people. Did he indulge in criticism? Oh, yes. As a young man in the Pigeon Creek Valley of Indiana, he not only criticized but he wrote letters and poems ridiculing people and dropped these letters on the country roads where they were sure to be found. One of these letters aroused resentments that burned for a lifetime.

Even after Lincoln had become a practising lawyer in Springfield, Illinois, he attacked his opponents openly in letters published in the newspapers. But he did this just once too often.

In the autumn of 1842 he ridiculed a vain, pugnacious politician by the name of James Shields. Lincoln lampooned him through an anonymous letter published in the Springfield *Journal.* The town roared with laughter. Shields, sensitive and proud, boiled with indignation. He found out who wrote the letter, leapt on his horse, started after Lincoln and challenged him to fight a duel. Lincoln didn't want to fight. He was opposed to duelling, but he couldn't get out of it and save his honor. He was given the choice of weapons. Since he had very long arms, he chose cavalry broadswords and took lessons in sword fighting from a West Point graduate; and, on the appointed day, he and Shields met on a sandbar in the Mississippi River, prepared to fight to the death; but, at the last minute, their seconds interrupted and stopped the duel.

That was the most lurid personal incident in Lincoln's life. It taught him an invaluable lesson in the art of dealing with people. Never again did he write an insulting letter. Never again did he ridicule anyone. And from that time on, he almost never criticized anybody for anything.

Time after time, during the Civil War, Lincoln put a new general at the head of the Army of the Potomac, and each one in turn—McClellan, Pope, Burnside, Hooker, Meade—blundered tragically and drove Lincoln to pacing the floor in despair. Half the nation savagely condemned these incompetent generals, but Lincoln, "with malice toward none, with charity for all," held his peace. One of his favourite quotations was: "Judge not, that ye be not judged."

And when Mrs. Lincoln and others spoke harshly of the

southern people, Lincoln replied: "Don't criticize them; they are just what we would be under similar circumstances."

Yet if any man ever had occasion to criticize, surely it was Lincoln. Let's take just one illustration:

The Battle of Gettysburg was fought during the first three days of July 1863. During the night of 4 July Lee began to retreat southward while storm clouds deluged the country with rain. When Lee reached the Potomac with his defeated army, he found a swollen, impassable river in front of him, and a victorious Union Army behind him. Lee was in a trap. He couldn't escape. Lincoln saw that. Here was a golden, heaven-sent opportunity—the opportunity to capture Lee's army and end the war immediately. So, with a surge of hope, Lincoln ordered Meade not to call a council of war but to attack Lee immediately. Lincoln telegraphed his orders and then sent a special messenger to Meade demanding immediate action.

And what did General Meade do? He did the very opposite of what he was told to do. He called a council of war in direct violation of Lincoln's orders. He hesitated. He procrastinated. He telegraphed all manner of excuses. He refused point-blank to attack Lee. Finally the waters receded and Lee escaped over the Potomac with his forces.

Lincoln was furious. "What does this mean?" Lincoln cried to his son Robert. "Great God! What does this mean? We had them within our grasp, and had only to stretch forth our hands and they were ours; yet nothing that I could say or do could make the army move. Under the circumstances, almost any general could have defeated Lee. If I had gone up there, I could have whipped him myself."

In bitter disappointment, Lincoln sat down and wrote Meade this letter. And remember, at this period of his life Lincoln was extremely conservative and restrained in his phraseology. So this letter coming from Lincoln in 1863 was tantamount to the severest rebuke.

My dear General,

> I do not believe you appreciate the magnitude of the misfortune involved in Lee's escape. He was within our easy grasp, and to have closed upon him would, in connection with our other late successes, have ended the war. As it is, the war will be prolonged indefinitely. If you could not safely attack Lee last Monday, how can you possibly do so south of the river, when you can take with you very few—no more than two-thirds of the force you then had in hand? It would be unreasonable to expect and I do not expect that you can now effect much. Your golden opportunity is gone, and I am distressed immeasurably because of it.

What do you suppose Meade did when he read the letter?

Meade never saw that letter. Lincoln never mailed it. It was found among his papers after his death.

My guess is—and this is only a guess—that after writing that letter, Lincoln looked out of the window and said to himself, "Just a minute. Maybe I ought not to be so hasty. It is easy enough for me to sit here in the quiet of the White House and order Meade to attack; but if I had been up at Gettysburg, and if I had seen as much blood as Meade has seen during the last week, and if my ears had been pierced with the screams and shrieks of the wounded and dying, maybe I wouldn't be so anxious to attack either. If I had Meade's timid temperament, perhaps I would have done just what he had done. Anyhow, it is water under the bridge now. If I send this letter, it will relieve my feelings, but it will make Meade try to justify himself. It will make him condemn me. It will arouse hard feelings, impair all his further usefulness as a commander, and perhaps force him to resign from the army."

So, as I have already said, Lincoln put the letter aside, for he had learnt by bitter experience that sharp criticisms and rebukes almost invariably end in futility.

FUTILITY OF CURT CRITICISM

Theodore Roosevelt said that when he, as President, was confronted with a perplexing problem, he used to lean back and look up at a large painting of Lincoln which hung above his desk in the White House and ask himself, "What would Lincoln do if he were in my shoes? How would he solve this problem?"

Mark Twain lost his temper occasionally and wrote letters that turned the paper brown. For example, he once wrote to a man who had aroused his ire: "The thing for you is a burial permit. You have only to speak and I will see that you get it." On another occasion he wrote to an editor about a proofreader's attempts to "improve my spelling and punctuation." He ordered: "Set the matter according to my copy hereafter and see that the proofreader retains his suggestions in the mush of his decayed brain."

The writing of these stinging letters made Mark Twain feel better. They allowed him to blow off steam, and the letters didn't do any real harm, because Mark's wife secretly lifted them out of the mail. They were never sent.

Do you know someone you would like to change and regulate and improve? Good! That is fine. I am all in favor of it. But why not begin on yourself? From a purely selfish standpoint, that is a lot more profitable than trying to improve others—yes, and a lot less dangerous. "Don't complain about the snow on your neighbor's roof," said Confucious, "when your own doorstep is unclean."

When I was still young and trying to impress people, I wrote a foolish letter to Richard Harding Davis, an author who once loomed large on the literary horizon of America. I was preparing a magazine article about authors, and I asked Davis to tell me about his method of work. A few weeks earlier, I had received a letter from someone with this notation at the bottom: "Dictated but not read." I was quite impressed. I felt that the writer must be very big and busy and important. I wasn't the slightest bit busy, but I was eager to make an impression on Richard Harding Davis, so I ended my short note with the words: "Dictated but not read."

He never troubled to answer the letter. He simply returned it to me with this scribbled across the bottom: "Your bad manners are exceeded only by your bad manners." True, I had blundered, and perhaps I deserved this rebuke. But, being human, I resented it. I resented it so sharply that when I read of the death of Richard Harding Davis ten years later, the one thought that still persisted in my mind—I am ashamed to admit—was the hurt he had given me.

If you and I want to stir up a resentment tomorrow that may rankle across the decades and endure until death, just let us indulge in a little stinging criticism—no matter how certain we are that it is justified.

When dealing with people, let us remember we are not dealing with creatures of logic. We are dealing with creatures of emotion, creatures bristling with prejudices and motivated by pride and vanity.

Bitter criticism caused the sensitive Thomas Hardy, one of the finest novelists ever to enrich English literature, to give up forever the writing of fiction. Criticism drove Thomas Chatterton, the English poet, to suicide.

Benjamin Franklin, tactless in his youth, became so diplomatic, so adroit at handling people, that he was made American Ambassador to France. The secret of his success? "I will speak ill of no man," he said, "…and speak all the good I know of everybody."

Any fool can criticize, condemn and complain—and most fools do.

But it takes character and self-control to be understanding and forgiving.

"A great man shows his greatness," said Carlyle, "by the way he treats little men."

Bob Hoover, a famous test pilot and frequent performer at air shows, was returning to his home in Los Angeles from an air show in San Diego. As described in the magazine *Flight Operations*, at 300 feet in the air, both engines suddenly stopped. By deft manoeuvring he managed to land the plane, but it was badly damaged although nobody was hurt.

Hoover's first act after the emergency landing was to inspect the aeroplane's fuel. Just as he suspected, the World War II propeller plane he had been flying had been fuelled with jet fuel rather than gasoline.

Upon returning to the airport, he asked to see the mechanic who had serviced his aeroplane. The young man was sick with the agony of his mistake. Tears streamed down his face as Hoover approached. He had just caused the loss of a very expensive plane and could have caused the loss of three lives as well.

You can imagine Hoover's anger. One could anticipate the tongue-lashing that this proud and precise pilot would unleash for that carelessness. But Hoover didn't scold the mechanic; he didn't even criticize him. Instead, he put his big arm around the man's shoulder and said, "To show you I'm sure that you'll never do this again, I want you to service my F-51 tomorrow."

Often parents are tempted to criticise their children. You would expect me to say "don't". But I will not. I am merely going to say, "*Before* you criticize them, read one of the classics of American journalism, 'Father Forgets.'" It originally appeared as an editorial in the *People's Home Journal*. We are reprinting it here with the author's permission, as condensed in the *Reader's Digest*:

'Father Forgets' is one of those little pieces which—dashed off in a moment of sincere feeling—strikes an echoing chord in so many readers as to become a perennial reprint favourite. Since its first appearance, 'Father Forgets' has been reproduced, writes the author, W. Livingstone Larned, "In hundreds of magazines and house organs, and in newspapers the country over. It has been reprinted almost as extensively in many foreign languages. I have given personal permission to thousands who wished to read it from school, church, and lecture platforms. It has been 'on the air' on countless occasions and programmes. Oddly enough, college periodicals have used it, and high-school magazines. Sometimes a little piece seems mysteriously to 'click'. This one certainly did."

FATHER FORGETS
W. Livingston Larned

Listen, son: I am saying this as you lie asleep, one little paw crumpled under your cheek and the blond curls stickily wet on your damp forehead. I have stolen into your room alone. Just a few minutes ago, as I sat reading my paper in the library, a stifling wave of remorse swept over me. Guiltily I came to your bedside.

There are the things I was thinking, son: I had been cross to you. I scolded you as you were dressing for school because you gave your face merely a dab with a towel. I took you to task for not cleaning your shoes. I called out angrily when you threw some of your things on the floor.

At breakfast I found fault, too. You spilled things. You gulped down your food. You put your elbows on the table. You spread butter too thick on your bread. And as you started off to play and I made for my train, you turned and waved a hand and called, "Goodbye, Daddy!" and I frowned, and said in reply, "Hold your shoulders back!"

Then it began all over again in the late afternoon. As I came up the road I spied you, down on your knees, playing marbles. There were holes in your stockings. I humiliated you before your boyfriends by marching you ahead of me to the house. Stockings were expensive— and if you had to buy them you would be more careful! Imagine that, son, from a father!

Do you remember, later, when I was reading in the library, how you came in timidly, with a sort of hurt look in your eyes? When I glanced up over my paper, impatient at the interruption, you hesitated at the door. "What is it you want?" I snapped.

You said nothing, but ran across in one tempestuous plunge, and threw your arms around my neck and kissed me, and your small arms tightened with an affection that God had set blooming in your heart and which even neglect could not wither. And then you were gone, pattering up the stairs.

Well, son, it was shortly afterwards that my paper slipped from my hands and a terrible sickening fear came over me. What has habit been doing to me? The habit of finding fault, of reprimanding—this was my reward to you for being a boy. It was not that I did not love you; it was that I expected too much of youth. I was measuring you by the yardstick of my own years.

And there was so much that was good and fine and true in your character. The little heart of you was as big as the dawn itself over the wide hills. This was shown by your spontaneous impulse to rush in and kiss me good night. Nothing else matters tonight, son. I have come to your bedside in the darkness, and I have knelt there, ashamed!

It is a feeble atonement; I know you would not understand these things if I told them to you during your waking hours. But tomorrow I will be a real daddy! I will chum with you, and suffer when you suffer, and laugh when you laugh. I will bite my tongue when impatient words come. I will keep saying as if it were a ritual: "He is nothing but a boy—a little boy!"

I am afraid I have visualized you as a man. Yet as I see you now, son, crumpled and weary in your cot, I see that you are still a baby. Yesterday you were in your mother's arms, your head on her shoulder. I have asked too much, too much.

Instead of condemning people, let's try to understand them. Let's try to figure out why they do what they do. That's a lot more profitable and intriguing than criticism; and it breeds sympathy, tolerance and kindness. "To know all is to forgive all."

As Dr. Johnson said: "God himself, sir, does not propose to judge man until the end of his days."

Why should you and I?

POINTS TO REMEMBER

1. The futility of criticism.
2. Aim to change yourself first, and then others.
3. Parental guide on correcting children.

10

HOW TO MAKE YOUR MEANING CLEAR

A famous English bishop, during the last war, spoke to some unlettered negro troops. They were on their way to the trenches; but a very small percentage of them had any adequate idea why they were being sent. I know: I questioned them. Yet the Lord Bishop talked to these negroes about "international amity" and "Servia's right to a place in the sun". Why, the half of those negroes did not know whether Servia was a town or a disease. He might as well, as far as results were concerned, have delivered a sonorous eulogy on the Nebular Hypothesis. However, not a single trooper left the hall while he was speaking: the military police with revolvers were stationed at every exit to prevent that consummation.

I do not wish to belittle the bishop. He is every inch a scholar, and before a body of collegiate men he would probably have been powerful, but he failed with these negroes, and he failed utterly: he did not know his audience, and he evidently knew neither the precise purpose of his talk nor how to accomplish it.

What do we mean by the purpose of an address? Just this: every talk, regardless of whether the speaker realizes it or not, has one of four major goals. What are they?

1. To make something clear.
2. To impress and convince.
3. To get action.
4. To entertain.

Let us illustrate these by a series of concrete examples.

Lincoln, who was always more or less interested in mechanics, once invented and patented a device for lifting stranded boats off sand bars and other obstructions. He worked in a mechanic's shop near his law office, making a model of his apparatus. Although the device finally came to naught, he was decidedly enthusiastic over its possibilities. When friends came to his office to view the model, he took no end of pains to explain it. The main purpose of those explanations was clearness.

When he delivered his immortal oration at Gettysburg, when he gave his first and second inaugural addresses, when Henry Clay died and Lincoln delivered an eulogy on his life—on all these occasions, Lincoln's main purpose was impressiveness and conviction. He had to be clear, of course, because he could be convincing; but, in these instances, clearness was not his major consideration.

In his talks to juries, he tried to win favourable decisions. In his political talks, he tried to win votes. His purpose, then, was *action*.

Two years before he was elected President, Lincoln prepared a lecture on Inventions. His purpose was entertainment. At least, that should have been his goal, but he was evidently not very successful in attaining it. His career as a popular lecturer was, in fact, a distinct disappointment. In one town, not a person came to hear him.

But he did succeed and he succeeded famously in the other speeches of his that I have referred to. And why? Because, in those instances, he knew his goal, and he knew how to achieve it. He knew where he wanted to go and how to get there. And because so many speakers don't know just that, they often flounder and come to grief.

For example: I once saw a United States Congressman hooted and hissed and forced to leave the stage of the old New York Hippodrome, because he had—unconsciously, no doubt, but nevertheless, unwisely—chosen clearness as his goal. It was during the last war. He talked to his audience about how the United States was preparing. The crowd did not want to be instructed. They wanted to be entertained. They listened to him patiently, politely, for ten minutes, a quarter of an hour, hoping the performance would come to a rapid end. But it didn't. He rambled on and on; patience snapped and the audience would not stand for more. Someone began to cheer ironically. Others took it up. In a moment, a thousand people were whistling and shouting. The speaker, obtuse and incapable as he was of sensing the temper of his audience, had the bad taste to continue. That aroused them. A battle was on. Their impatience mounted to ire. They determined to silence him. Louder and louder grew their storm of protest. Finally, the roar of it, the anger of it drowned his words—he could not have been heard twenty feet away. So he was forced to give up, acknowledge defeat, and retire in humiliation.

Profit by his example. Know your goal. Choose it wisely before you set out to prepare your talk. Know how to reach it. Then set about it, doing it skillfully and with science.

All this requires knowledge, special and technical instruction. The remainder of this chapter will show you how to make your talks clear.

USE COMPARISONS TO PROMOTE CLEARNESS

As to clearness: do not underestimate the importance of it nor the difficulty. I recently heard a certain Irish poet give an evening of readings from his own poems. Not 10 per cent of the audience, half the time, knew what he was talking about. Many talkers, both in public and private, are a lot like that.

When I discussed the essentials of public speaking with Sir Oliver Lodge, a man who has been lecturing to university classes and to the public for forty years, he emphasized most of all the importance, first, of knowledge and preparation, and second, of "taking good pains to be clear".

The great General Von Moltke, at the outbreak of the Franco-Prussian War, said to his officers: "Remember, gentlemen, that any order that *can* be misunderstood, *will* be misunderstood."

Napoleon recognized the same danger. His most emphatic and oft-reiterated instruction to his secretaries was: "Be clear! Be clear!"

When the disciples asked Christ why He taught the public by parables, He answered: "Because they seeing, see not: and hearing, hear not; neither do they understand."

And when you talk on a subject strange to your hearer or hearers, can you hope that they will understand you any more readily than people understood the Master?

Hardly. So what can we do about it? What did He do when confronted by a similar situation? Solved it in the most simple and natural manner imaginable: described the things people did not know by likening them to things they did know. The kingdom of Heaven...what would it be like? How could those untutored peasants of Palestine know? So Christ described it in terms of objects and actions with which they were already familiar:

The kingdom of Heaven is like unto leaven, which a woman took, and hid in three measures of meal, till the whole was leavened.

Again, the kingdom of Heaven is like unto a merchantman seeking goodly pearls...

Again, the kingdom of Heaven is like unto a net that was cast into the sea...

That was lucid; they could understand that. The housewives in the audience were using leaven every week; the fishermen were casting their nets into the sea daily; the merchants were dealing in pearls.

And how did David make clear the watchfulness and loving kindness of Jehovah?

"The Lord is my shepherd, I shall not want. He maketh me to lie down in green pastures, He leadeth me beside the still waters..."

Green grazing grounds in that almost barren country... still waters where the sheep could drink—those pastoral people could understand that.

Here is a rather striking and half-amusing example of the use of this principle: some missionaries were translating the Bible into the dialect of a tribe near equatorial Africa. They progressed to the verse: "Though your sins be as scarlet, they shall be white as snow." How were they to translate that? Literally? Meaningless. Absurd. The natives had never scooped snow off the pathway on a February morning. They did not even have a word for snow. They could not have told the difference between snow and coal tar, but they had climbed coconut trees many times and shaken down a few nuts for lunch; so the missionaries likened the unknown to the known, and changed the verse to read: "Though your sins be as scarlet, they shall be as white as the meat of a coconut."

Under the circumstances, it would be hard to improve on that, wouldn't it?

At a Teachers' College, I once heard a lecturer on Alaska who failed, in many places, to be either clear or interesting because, unlike those African missionaries, he neglected to talk in terms of what his audience knew. He told us, for example, that Alaska had a gross area of 590,804 square miles, and a population of 64,356.

Half a million square miles—what does that mean to the average man? Precious little. He is not used to thinking in terms of square miles. They conjure up no mental picture. Suppose the speaker had said that the coastline of Alaska and its islands is longer than the distance around the globe, and that its area more than equals the combined areas of Vermont, New Hampshire, Maine, Massachusetts, Rhode Island, Connecticut, New York, New Jersey, Pennsylvania, Delaware, Maryland, West Virginia, North Carolina, South Carolina, Georgia, Florida, Mississippi and Tennessee. Would not that give everyone a fairly clear conception of the area of Alaska?

He said the population was 64,356. The chances are that not one person in ten remembered the census figures for five minutes—or even one minute. Why? Because the rapid saying of "sixty-four thousand, three hundred and fifty-six" does not make a very clear impression. It leaves only a loose, insecure impression, like words written on the sand of the seashore. The next wave of attention quite obliterates them. Would it not have been better to have stated the census in terms of something with which they were very familiar? Better still, why not talk about Alaska in terms of the very town where you are speaking?

In the following illustrations, which are the clearer, the (a) statement or the (b)?

(a) Our nearest star is thirty-five trillion miles away.

(b) A train going at the rate of a mile a minute would reach our nearest star in forty-eight million years; if a song were sung there and the sound could travel here it would be three million eight hundred thousand years before we could hear it. A spider's thread reaching to it would weigh five hundred tons.

(a) St. Peter's, the biggest church in the world, is 232 yards long, and 364 feet wide.

(b) It is about the size of two buildings like the capital at Washington piled on top of one another.

Sir Oliver Lodge happily uses this method when explaining the size and nature of atoms to a popular audience. I heard him tell a European audience that there were as many atoms in a drop of water as there were drops of water in the Mediterranean Sea; and many of his hearers had spent over a week sailing from Gibraltar to the Suez Canal. To bring the matter still closer home, he said there were as many atoms in one drop of water as there were blades of grass on all the earth.

Richard Harding Davis told a New York audience that the Mosque of St. Sophia was "about as big as the auditorium of the Fifth Avenue theatre". He said Brindisi "looks like Long Island City when you come into it from the rear."

Use this principle henceforth in your talks. If you are describing the great pyramid, first tell your hearers it is 451 feet, then tell them how high that is in terms of some building they see every day. Tell how many city blocks the base would cover. Don't speak about so many thousand gallons of this or so many hundred thousand barrels of that without also telling how many rooms the size of the one you are speaking in could be filled with that much liquid. Instead of saying twenty feet high, why not say one and a half times as high as this ceiling? Instead of talking about distance in terms of rods or miles, is it not clearer to say as far as from here to some station, or to such and such a street?

AVOID TECHNICAL TERMS

If you belong to a profession the work of which is technical—if you are a lawyer, a physician, an engineer, or are in a highly specialized line of business—be doubly careful when you talk to outsiders, to express yourself in plain terms and to give necessary details.

I say be doubly careful for, as a part of my professional duties, I have listened to hundreds of speeches that failed right at this point and failed woefully. The speakers appeared totally unconscious of the general public's widespread and profound ignorance regarding their particular specialties. So what happened? They rambled on and on, uttering thoughts, using phrases that fitted into their experience and were instantly and continuously meaningful to them; but to the uninitiated, they were about as clear as a river after the rains have fallen on the newly-ploughed cornfields along its banks.

What should such a speaker do? He ought to read and heed the following advice from the facile pen of ex-Senator Beveridge:

> It is a good practice to pick out the least intelligent looking person in the audience and strive to make that person interested in your argument. This can be done only by lucid statement of fact and clear reasoning. An even better method is to center your talk on some small boy or girl present with parents.

Say to yourself—say out loud to your audience, if you like—that you will try to be so plain that the child will understand and remember your explanation of the question discussed, and after the meeting be able to tell what you have said.

THE SECRET TO LINCOLN'S CLEARNESS

Lincoln had a deep and abiding affection for putting a proposition so that it would be instantly clear to everyone. In his first message to Congress, he used the phrase "sugar-coated". Mr. Defrees, the public printer, being Lincoln's personal friend, suggested to him that although the phrase might be all right for a stump speech in Illinois, it was not dignified enough for a historical state paper. "Well, Defrees," Lincoln replied, "if you think the time will ever come when the people will not understand what 'sugar-coated' means, I'll alter it; otherwise, I think I'll let it go."

He once explained to Dr. Gulliver, the President of Knox College, how he developed his "passion" for plain language, as he phrased it:

Among my earliest recollections I remember how, when a mere child. I used to get irritated when anybody talked to me in a way I could not understand. I don't think I ever got angry at anything else in my life. But that always disturbed my temper, and has ever since. I can remember going to my little bedroom, after hearing the neighbors talk of an evening with my father, and spending no small part of the night walking up and down and trying to make out the exact meaning of some of their, to me, dark sayings. I could not sleep, though I often tried to, when

I got on such a hunt after an idea, until I had caught it, and when I thought I had got it I was not satisfied until I had repeated it over and over, until I had put it in language plain enough as I thought for any boy I knew to comprehend. This was a kind of passion with me, and it has since stuck by me.

A passion? Yes, it must have amounted to that, for Mentor Graham, the schoolmaster of New Salem, testified: "I have known Lincoln to study for hours the best way of three to express an idea."

An all too common reason why men fail to be intelligible is this: the thing they wish to express is not clear even to themselves. Hazy impressions! Indistinct, vague ideas! The result? Their minds work no better in a mental fog than a camera does in a physical fog. They need to be as disturbed over obscurity and ambiguity as Lincoln was. They need to use his methods.

APPEAL TO THE SENSE OF SIGHT

The nerves that lead from the eye to the brain are many times larger than those leading from the ear; and science tells us that we give twenty-five times as much attention to eye suggestions as we do to ear suggestions.

"One seeing," says an old Japanese proverb, "is better than a hundred times telling about."

So, if you wish to be clear, picture your points, visualize your ideas. That was the plan of the late John H. Patterson, President of the well-known National Cash Register Company. He wrote an article for *System Magazine*, outlining the methods he used in speaking to his workmen and his sales forces:

I hold that one cannot rely on speech alone to make himself understood or to gain and hold attention. A dramatic supplement is needed. It is better to supplement whenever possible with pictures which show the right and the wrong way; diagrams are more convincing than mere words, and pictures are more convincing than diagrams. The ideal presentation of a subject is one in which every sub-division is pictured and in which the words are used only to connect them. I early found that in dealing with men, a picture was worth more than anything I could say.

Little grotesque drawings are wonderfully effective… I have a whole system of cartooning or "chart talks". A circle with a dollar mark means a piece of money, a bag marked with a dollar is a lot of money. Many good effects can be had with moon faces. Draw a circle, put in a few dashes for the eyes, nose, mouth, and ears. Twisting these lines gives the expressions. The out-of-date man has the corner of his mouth down; the chipper, up-to-date fellow has the curves up. The drawings are homely, but the most effective cartoonists are not the men who make the prettiest pictures; the thing is to express the idea and the contrast.

The big bag and the little bag of money, side by side, are the natural heads for the right way as opposed to the wrong way; the one brings much money, the other little money. If you sketch these rapidly as you talk, there is no danger of people's letting their minds wander; they are bound to look at what you are doing and thus to go with you through the successive stages to the point you want to make. And again, the funny figures put people in good humor.

I used to employ an artist to hang around in the shops with me and quietly make sketches of things that were not being done right. Then the sketches were made into drawings and I called the men together and showed them exactly what they were doing. When I heard of the stereopticon I immediately bought one and projected the drawings on the screen, which, of course, made them even more effective than on paper. Then came the moving picture. I think that I had one of the first machines ever made and now we have a big department with many motion picture films and more than 60,000 coloured stereopticon slides.

Not every subject or occasion, of course, lends itself to exhibits and drawings; but let us use them when we can. They attract attention, stimulate interest and often make our meaning doubly clear.

ROCKEFELLER RAKING OFF THE COINS

Mr. Rockefeller also used the columns of *System Magazine* to tell how he appealed to the sense of sight to make clear the financial situation of the Colorado Fuel and Iron Company:

I found that they (the employees of the Colorado Fuel and Iron Co.) imagined the Rockefellers had been drawing immense profits from their interests in Colorado; no end of people had told them so. I explained the exact situation to them. I showed them that during the fourteen years in which we had been connected with the Colorado Fuel and Iron Co., it had never paid one cent in dividends upon the common stock.

At one of our meetings, I gave a practical illustration of the finances of the company. I put a number of coins on the table. I swept off a portion which represented their wages—for the first claim upon the company is the payroll. Then I took away more coins to represent the salaries of the officers, and then the remaining coins to represent the fees of the directors. There were no coins left for the stockholders. And when I asked: "Men, is it fair, in this corporation where we are all partners, that three of the partners should get all the earnings, be they large or small—all of them—and the fourth nothing?"

After the illustration, one of the men made a speech for higher wages. I asked him, "Is it fair for you to want more wages when one of the partners gets nothing?" He admitted that it did not look like a square deal; I heard no more about increasing the wages.

Make your eye appeals definite and specific. Paint mental pictures that stand out as sharp and clear as a stag's horn silhouetted against the setting sun. For example, the word "dog" calls up a more or less definite picture of such an animal—perhaps a cocker spaniel, a Scotch terrier, a St. Bernard, or a Pomeranian. Notice how much more distinct an image springs into your mind when I say "bulldog"—the term is less inclusive. Doesn't "a brindle bulldog" call up a still more explicit picture? Is it not more vivid to say "a black Shetland pony" than to talk of "a horse"? Doesn't "a white bantam rooster with a broken leg" give a much more definite and sharp picture than merely the word "fowl"?

RESTATE YOUR IMPORTANT IDEAS IN DIFFERENT WORDS

Napoleon declared repetition to be the only serious principle of rhetoric. He knew that because an idea which was clear to him was not always proof that it was instantly grasped by others. He knew that it takes time to comprehend new ideas, that the mind must be kept focused on them. In short, he knew they must be repeated. Not in exactly the same language. People will rebel at that, and rightly so. But if the repetition is couched in fresh phraseology, if it is varied, your hearers will never regard it as repetition at all.

Let us take a specific example. The late Mr. Bryan said: "You cannot make people understand a subject, unless you understand that subject yourself. The more clearly you have a subject in mind, the more clearly can you present that subject to the minds of others."

The last sentence here is merely a restatement of the idea contained in the first, but when these sentences are spoken, the mind does not have time to see that it is repetition. It only *feels* that the subject has been made more clear.

I seldom teach a single session of this course without hearing one or perhaps half a dozen talks that would have been more clear, more impressive, had the speaker but employed this principle of restatement. It is almost entirely ignored by the beginner. And what a pity!

USE GENERAL ILLUSTRATIONS AND SPECIFIC INSTANCES

One of the surest and easiest ways to make your points clear is to follow them with general illustrations and concrete cases. What is the difference between the two? One, as the term implies, is general; the other, specific.

Let us illustrate the difference between them and the uses of each with a concrete example. Suppose we take the statement: "There are professional men and women who earn astonishingly large incomes."

Is that statement very clear? Have you a clearcut idea of what the speaker really means? No, and the speaker himself cannot be sure of what such an assertion will call up in the minds of others. It may cause the country doctor to think of a family doctor in a small city with an income of five thousand. It may cause a successful mining engineer to think in terms of the men in his profession who make a hundred thousand a year. The statement, as it stands, is entirely too vague and loose. It needs to be tightened. A few illuminating details ought to be given to indicate what professions the speaker refers to and what he means by "astonishingly large".

"There are lawyers, prize-fighters, song-writers, novelists, playwrights, painters, actors and singers who make more than the President of the United States."

Now, hasn't one a much clearer idea of what the speaker meant? However, he has not individualized. He has used general illustrations, not specific instances. He has said "singers", not Rosa Ponselle, Kirsten Flagstad, or Lily Pons.

So the statement is still more or less vague. We cannot call up concrete cases to illustrate it. Should not the speaker do it for us? Would he not be clearer if he employed specific examples—as is done in the following paragraph:

The great trial lawyers Samuel Untermeyer and Max Steuer earn as much as one million dollars a year. Jack Dempsey's annual income has been known to be as high as a half-million dollars. Joe Louis, the young, uneducated negro pugilist, while still in his twenties, has earned more than a half-million dollars. Irving Berlin's rag-time music is reported to have brought him a half million dollars yearly. Sidney Kingsley has made ten thousand dollars a week royalty on his plays. H.G. Wells has admitted, in his autobiography, that his pen has brought him three million dollars. Diego Rivera has earned, from his paintings, more than half a million dollars in a year. Katherine Cornell has repeatedly refused five thousand dollars a week to go into pictures. Lawrence Tibbet and Grace Moore are reported to have an annual income of a quarter-million dollars.

Now, has not one an extremely plain and vivid idea of exactly and precisely what the speaker wanted to convey?

Be concrete. Be definite. Be specific. This quality of definiteness not only makes for clearness but for impressiveness and conviction and interest also.

DO NOT EMULATE THE MOUNTAIN GOAT

Professor William James, in one of his talks to teachers, pauses to remark that one can make only one point in a lecture, and the lecture he referred to lasted an hour. Yet I recently heard a speaker, who was limited by a stopwatch to three minutes, begin by saying that he wanted to call our attention to eleven points. Sixteen and a half seconds to each phase of his subject! Seems incredible, doesn't it, that an intelligent man should attempt anything so manifestly absurd. True, I am quoting an extreme case, but the tendency to err in that fashion, if not to that degree, handicaps almost every novice. He is like a Cook's guide who shows Paris to the tourist in one day. It can be done, just as one can walk through the Museum of Natural History in thirty minutes. But neither clearness nor enjoyment results. Many a talk fails to be clear because the speaker seems intent upon establishing a world's record for ground covered in the allotted time. He leaps from one point to another with the swiftness and agility of a mountain goat.

The talks in this course must, owing to the pressure of time, be short; so cut your cloth accordingly. If, for example, you are to speak on Labor Unions, do not attempt to tell us in three or six minutes why they came into existence, the methods they employ, the good they have accomplished, the evil they have wrought, and how to solve industrial disputes. No, no; if you strive to do that, no one will have a very clear conception of what you have said. It will be all confused, a blur, too sketchy, too much of a mere outline.

Wouldn't it be the part of wisdom to take one phase and one phase only of labor unions, and cover that adequately and illustrate it? It would. That kind of speech leaves a single impression. It is lucid, easy to listen to, easy to remember.

However, if you must cover several phases of your topic, it is often advisable to summarize briefly at the end. Let us see how that suggestion operates. Here is a summary of this lesson. Does the reading of it help to make the message we have been presenting more lucid, more comprehensible?

POINTS TO REMEMBER

1. Know your audience.
2. Use plain language to avoid technical jargons
3. Identify your goal as a speaker and stick to it.

11

THE TRUTH ABOUT GESTURE

Gesture is really a simple matter that requires observation and common sense rather than a book of rules. Gesture is an outward expression of an inward condition. It is merely an effect—the effect of a mental or an emotional impulse struggling for expression through physical avenues.

You must not, however, begin at the wrong end: if you are troubled by your gestures, or a lack of gestures, attend to the cause, not the effect. It will not in the least help matters to tack on to your delivery a few mechanical movements. If the tree in your front yard is not growing to suit you, fertilize and water the soil and let the tree have sunshine. Obviously it will not help your tree to nail on a few branches. If your cistern is dry, wait until it rains; or bore a well. Why plunge a pump into a dry hole?

The speaker whose thoughts and emotions are welling within him like a mountain spring will not have much trouble to make gestures; it will be merely a question of properly directing them. If his enthusiasm for his subject is not such as to give him a natural impulse for dramatic action, it will avail nothing to furnish him with a long list of rules. He may tack on some movements, but they will look like the wilted branches nailed to a tree to simulate life. Gestures must be born, not built. A wooden horse may amuse the children, but it takes a live one to go somewhere.

It is not only impossible to lay down definite rules on this subject, but it would be silly to try, for everything depends on the speech, the occasion, the personality and feelings of the speaker, and the attitude of the audience. It is easy enough to forecast the result of multiplying seven by six, but it is impossible to tell any man what kind of gestures he will be impelled to use when he wishes to show his earnestness. We may tell him that many speakers close the hand, with the exception of the forefinger, and pointing that finger straight at the audience pour out their thoughts like a volley; or that others stamp one foot for emphasis; or that Mr Bryan often slaps his hands together for great force, holding one palm upward in an easy manner; or that Gladstone would sometimes make a rush at the clerk's table in Parliament and smite it with his hand so forcefully that Disraeli once brought down the house by grimly congratulating himself that such a barrier stood between himself and "the honorable gentleman."

All these things, and a bookful more, may we tell the speaker, but we cannot know whether he can use these gestures or not, any more than we can decide whether he could wear Mr. Bryan's clothes. The best that can be done on this subject is to offer a few practical suggestions, and let personal good taste decide as to where effective dramatic action ends and extravagant motion begins.

ANY GESTURE THAT MERELY CALLS ATTENTION TO ITSELF IS BAD

The purpose of a gesture is to carry your thought and feeling into the minds and hearts of your hearers; this it does by emphasizing your message, by interpreting it, by expressing it in action, by striking its tone in either a physically descriptive, a suggestive, or a typical gesture—and let it be remembered all the time that gesture includes all physical movement, from facial expression and the tossing of the head to the expressive movements of hand and foot. A shifting of the pose may be a most effective gesture.

What is true of gesture is true of all life. If the people on the street turn around and watch your walk, your walk is more important than you are—change it. If the attention of your audience is called to your gestures, they are not convincing, because they appear to be—what they have a doubtful right to be in reality—studied. Have you ever seen a speaker use such grotesque gesticulations that you were fascinated by their frenzy of oddity, but could not follow his thought? Do not smother ideas with gymnastics. Savonarola would rush down from the high pulpit among the congregation in the duomo at Florence and carry the fire of conviction to his hearers; Billy Sunday slides to base on the platform carpet in dramatizing one of his baseball illustrations. Yet in both instances the message has somehow stood out bigger than the gesture—it is chiefly in calm afterthought that men have remembered the form of dramatic expression. When Sir Henry Irving made his famous exit as Shylock, the last thing the audience saw was his pallid, avaricious hand extended skinny and claw-like against the background. At the time, every one was overwhelmed by the tremendous typical quality of this gesture; now, we have time to think of its art, and discuss its realistic power.

Only when gesture is subordinated to the absorbing importance of the idea—a spontaneous, living expression of living truth—is it justifiable at all; and when it is remembered for itself—as a piece of unusual physical energy or as a poem of grace—it is a dead failure as dramatic expression. There is a place for a unique style of walking—it is the circus or the cake-walk; there is a place for surprisingly rhythmical evolutions of arms and legs—it is on the dance floor or the stage. Don't let your agility and grace put your thoughts out of business.

One of the present writers took his first lesson in gesture from a certain college president who knew far more about what had happened at the Diet of Worms than he did about how to express himself in action. His instructions were to start the movement on a certain word, continue it on a precise curve, and unfold the fingers at the conclusion, ending with the forefinger—just so. Plenty, and more than plenty, has been published on this subject, giving just such silly directions. Gesture is a thing of mentality and feeling—not a matter of geometry. Remember, whenever a pair of shoes, a method of pronunciation, or a gesture calls attention to itself, it is bad. When you have made really good gestures in a good speech your hearers will not go away saying, "What beautiful gestures he made!" but they will say, "I'll vote for that measure." "He is right—I believe in that."

GESTURES SHOULD BE BORN OF THE MOMENT

The best actors and public speakers rarely know in advance what gestures they are going to make. They make one gesture on certain words tonight, and none at all tomorrow night at the same point—their various moods and interpretations govern their gestures. It is all a matter of impulse and intelligent feeling with them—don't overlook that word intelligent. Nature does not always provide the same kind of sunsets or snow flakes, and the movements of a good speaker vary almost as much as the creations of nature.

Now all this is not to say that you must not take some thought for your gestures. If that were meant, why this chapter? When the sergeant despairingly besought the recruit in the awkward squad to step out and look at himself, he gave splendid advice—and worthy of personal application. Particularly while you are in the learning days of public speaking you must learn to criticise your own gestures. Recall them—see where they were useless, crude, awkward, what not, and do better next time. There is a vast deal of difference between being conscious of self and being self-conscious.

It will require your nice discrimination in order to cultivate spontaneous gestures and yet give due attention to practice. While you depend upon the moment it is vital to remember that only a dramatic genius can effectively accomplish such feats as we have related of Whitefield, Savonarola, and others: and doubtless the first time they were used they came in a burst of spontaneous feeling, yet Whitefield declared that not until he had delivered a sermon forty times was its delivery perfected. What spontaneity initiates, let practice complete. Every effective speaker and every vivid actor has observed, considered and practiced gesture until his dramatic actions are a sub-conscious possession, just like his ability to pronounce correctly without especially concentrating his thought. Every able platform man has possessed himself of a dozen ways in which he might depict in gesture any given emotion; in fact, the means for such expression are endless—and this is precisely why it is both useless and harmful to make a chart of gestures and enforce them as the ideals of what may be used to express this or that feeling. Practice descriptive, suggestive, and typical movements until they come as naturally as a good articulation; and rarely forecast the gestures you will use at a given moment: leave something to that moment.

AVOID MONOTONY IN GESTURE

Roast beef is an excellent dish, but it would be terrible as an exclusive diet. No matter how effective one gesture is, do not overwork it. Put variety in your actions. Monotony will destroy all beauty and power. The pump handle makes one effective gesture, and on hot days that one is very eloquent, but it has its limitations.

ANY MOVEMENT THAT IS NOT SIGNIFICANT, WEAKENS

Do not forget that. Restlessness is not expression. A great many useless movements will only take the attention of the audience from what you are saying. A widely-noted man introduced the speaker of the evening one Sunday lately to a New York audience. The only thing remembered about that introductory speech is that the speaker played nervously with the covering of the table as he talked. We naturally watch moving objects. A janitor putting down a window can take the attention of the hearers from Mr. Roosevelt. By making a few movements at one side of the stage a chorus girl may draw the interest of the spectators from a big scene between the "leads." When our forefathers lived in caves they had to watch moving objects, for movements meant danger. We have not yet overcome the habit. Advertisers have taken advantage of it—witness the moving electric light signs in any city. A shrewd speaker will respect this law and conserve the attention of his audience by eliminating all unnecessary movements.

GESTURE SHOULD EITHER BE SIMULTANEOUS WITH OR PRECEDE THE WORDS—NOT FOLLOW THEM

Lady Macbeth says: "Bear welcome in your eye, your hand, your tongue." Reverse this order and you get comedy. Say, "There he goes," pointing at him after you have finished your words, and see if the result is not comical.

DO NOT MAKE SHORT, JERKY MOVEMENTS

Some speakers seem to be imitating a waiter who has failed to get a tip. Let your movements be easy, and from the shoulder, as a rule, rather than from the elbow. But do not go to the other extreme and make too many flowing motions—that savors of the lackadaisical.

Put a little "punch" and life into your gestures. You can not, however, do this mechanically. The audience will detect it if you do. They may not know just what is wrong, but the gesture will have a false appearance to them.

FACIAL EXPRESSION IS IMPORTANT

Have you ever stopped in front of a Broadway theater and looked at the photographs of the cast? Notice the row of chorus girls who are supposed to be expressing fear. Their attitudes are so mechanical that the attempt is ridiculous. Notice the picture of the "star" expressing the same emotion: his muscles are drawn, his eyebrows lifted, he shrinks, and fear shines through his eyes. That actor felt fear when the photograph was taken. The chorus girls felt that it was time for a rarebit, and more nearly expressed that emotion than they did fear. Incidentally, that is one reason why they stay in the chorus.

The movements of the facial muscles may mean a great deal more than the movements of the hand. The man who sits in a dejected heap with a look of despair on his face is expressing his thoughts and feelings just as effectively as the man who is waving his arms and shouting from the back of a dray wagon. The eye has been called the window of the soul. Through it shines the light of our thoughts and feelings.

DO NOT USE TOO MUCH GESTURE

As a matter of fact, in the big crises of life we do not go through many actions. When your closest friend dies you do not throw up your hands and talk about your grief. You are more likely to sit and brood in dry-eyed silence. The Hudson River does not make much noise on its way to the sea—it is not half so loud as the little creek up in Bronx Park that a bullfrog could leap across. The barking dog never tears your trousers—at least they say he doesn't. Do not fear the man who waves his arms and shouts his anger, but the man who comes up quietly with eyes flaming and face burning may knock you down. Fuss is not force. Observe these principles in nature and practice them in your delivery.

The writer of this chapter once observed an instructor drilling a class in gesture. They had come to the passage from Henry VIII in which the humbled Cardinal says: "Farewell, a long farewell to all my greatness." It is one of the pathetic passages of literature. A man uttering such a sentiment would be crushed, and the last thing on earth he would do would be to make flamboyant movements. Yet this class had an elocutionary manual before them that gave an appropriate gesture for every occasion, from paying the gas bill to death-bed farewells. So they were instructed to throw their arms out at full length on each side and say: "Farewell, a long farewell to all my greatness." Such a gesture might possibly be used in an after-dinner speech at the convention of a telephone company whose lines extended from the Atlantic to the Pacific, but to think of Wolsey's using that movement would suggest that his fate was just.

POSTURE

The physical attitude to be taken before the audience really is included in gesture. Just what that attitude should be depends, not on rules, but on the spirit of the speech and the occasion. Senator La Follette stood for three hours with his weight thrown on his forward foot as he leaned out over the footlights, ran his fingers through his hair, and flamed out a denunciation of the trusts. It was very effective. But imagine a speaker taking that kind of position to discourse on the development of road-making machinery. If you have a fiery, aggressive message, and will let yourself go, nature will naturally pull your weight to your forward foot. A man in a hot political argument or a street brawl never has to stop to think upon which foot he should throw his weight. You may sometimes place your weight on your back foot if you have a restful and calm message—but don't worry about it: just stand like a man who genuinely feels what he is saying. Do not stand with your heels close together, like a soldier or a butler. No more should you stand with them wide apart like a traffic policeman. Use simple good manners and common sense.

Here a word of caution is needed. We have advised you to allow your gestures and postures to be spontaneous and not woodenly prepared beforehand, but do not go to the extreme of ignoring the importance of acquiring mastery of your physical movements. A muscular hand made flexible by free movement, is far more likely to be an effective instrument in gesture than a stiff, pudgy bunch of fingers. If your shoulders are lithe and carried well, while your chest does not retreat from association with your chin, the chances of using good extemporaneous gestures are so much the better. Learn to keep the back of your neck touching your collar, hold your chest high, and keep down your waist measure.

So attention to strength, poise, flexibility, and grace of body are the foundations of good gesture, for they are expressions of vitality, and without vitality no speaker can enter the kingdom of power. When an awkward giant like Abraham Lincoln rose to the sublimest heights of oratory he did so because of the greatness of his soul—his very ruggedness of spirit and artless honesty were properly expressed in his gnarly body. The fire of character, of earnestness, and of message swept his hearers before him when the tepid words of an insincere Apollo would have left no effect. But be sure you are a second Lincoln before you despise the handicap of physical awkwardness.

"Ty" Cobb has confided to the public that when he is in a batting slump he even stands before a mirror, bat in hand, to observe the "swing" and "follow through" of his batting form. If you would learn to stand well before an audience, look at yourself in a mirror—but not too often. Practice walking and standing before the mirror so as to conquer awkwardness—not to cultivate a pose. Stand on the platform in the same easy manner that you would use before guests in a drawing-room. If your position is not graceful, make it so by dancing, gymnasium work, and by getting grace and poise in your mind.

Do not continually hold the same position. Any big change of thought necessitates a change of position. Be at home. There are no rules—it is all a matter of taste. While on the platform forget that you have any hands until you desire to use them—then remember them effectively. Gravity will take care of them. Of course, if you want to put them behind you, or fold them once in awhile, it is not going to ruin your speech. Thought and feeling are the big things in speaking—not the position of a foot or a hand. Simply put your limbs where you want them to be—you have a will, so do not neglect to use it.

Let us reiterate, do not despise practice. Your gestures and movements may be spontaneous and still be wrong. No matter how natural they are, it is possible to improve them.

It is impossible for anyone—even yourself—to criticize your gestures until after they are made. You can't prune a peach tree until it comes up; therefore speak much, and observe your own speech. While you are examining yourself, do not forget to study statuary and paintings to see how the great portrayers of nature have made their subjects express ideas through action. Notice the gestures of the best speakers and actors. Observe the physical expression of life everywhere. The leaves on the tree respond to the slightest breeze. The muscles of your face, the light of your eyes, should respond to the slightest change of feeling. Emerson says: "Every man that I meet is my superior in some way. In that I learn of him." Illiterate Italians make gestures so wonderful and beautiful that Booth or Barrett might have sat at their feet and been instructed. Open your eyes. Emerson says again: "We are immersed in beauty, but our eyes have no clear vision." Toss this book to one side; go out and watch one child plead with another for a bite of apple; see a street brawl; observe life in action. Do you want to know how to express victory? Watch the victors' hands go high on election night. Do you want to plead a cause? Make a composite photograph of all the pleaders in daily life you constantly see. Beg, borrow, and steal the best you can get, BUT DON'T

GIVE IT OUT AS THEFT. Assimilate it until it becomes a part of you—then let the expression come out.

POINTS TO REMEMBER

1. Good gestures aren't something you are inherently born with. They require work.
2. Restless movements appear unattractive.
3. Observe the gestures that famous speakers and actors make.

12

TALK ABOUT YOUR OWN MISTAKES FIRST

My niece, Josephine Carnegie, had come to New York to be my secretary. She was nineteen, had graduated from high school three years previously, and her business experience was a trifle more than zero. She became one of the most proficient secretaries west of Suez, but in the beginning, she was—well, susceptible to improvement. One day when I started to criticize her, I said to myself: "Just a minute, Dale Carnegie; just a minute. You are twice as old as Josephine. You have ten thousand times as much business experience. How can you possibly expect her to have your viewpoint, your judgment, your initiative—mediocre though they may be? And just a minute, Dale, what were you doing at nineteen? Remember the asinine mistakes and blunders you made? Remember the time you did this…and that…?"

After thinking the matter over, honestly and impartially, I concluded that Josephine's batting average at nineteen was better than mine had been—and that, I'm sorry to confess, isn't paying Josephine much of a compliment.

So after that, when I wanted to call Josephine's attention to a mistake, I used to begin by saying, "You have made a mistake,

Josephine, but the Lord knows, it's no worse than many I have made. You were not born with judgment. That comes only with experience, and you are better than I was at your age. I have been guilty of so many stupid, silly things myself, I have very little inclination to criticize you or anyone. But don't you think it would have been wiser if you had done so and so?"

It isn't nearly so difficult to listen to a recital of your faults if the person criticizing begins by humbly admitting that he, too, is far from impeccable.

E.G. Dillistone, an engineer in Brandon, Manitoba, Canada, was having problems with his new secretary. Letters he dictated were coming to his desk for signature with two or three spelling mistakes per page. Mr. Dillistone reported how he handled this:

"Like many engineers, I have not been noted for my excellent English or spelling. For years I have kept a little black thumb-index book for words I had trouble spelling. When it became apparent that merely pointing out the errors was not going to cause my secretary to do more proofreading and dictionary work, I resolved to take another approach. When the next letter came to my attention that had errors in it, I sat down with the typist and said:

"'Somehow this word doesn't look right. It's one of the words I always have had trouble with. That's the reason I started this spelling book of mine. (I opened the book to the appropriate page.) Yes, here it is. I'm very conscious of the spelling now because people do judge us by our letters, and misspellings make us look less professional.'

"I don't know whether she copied my system or not, but since that conversation, her frequency of spelling errors has been significantly reduced."

The polished Prince Bernhard von Bülow learned the sharp

necessity of doing this back in 1909. Von Bülow was then the imperial chancellor of Germany, and on the throne sat Wilhelm II—Wilhelm, the haughty; Wilhelm, the arrogant; Wilhelm, the last of the German kaisers, building an army and navy that he boasted could whip their weight in wildcats.

Then an astonishing thing happened. The kaiser said things, incredible things, things that rocked the continent and started a series of explosions heard around the world. To make matters worse, the kaiser made silly, egotistical, absurd announcements in public. He made them while he was a guest in England, and he gave his royal permission to have them printed in the *Daily Telegraph*. For example, he declared that he was the only German who felt friendly toward the English; that he was constructing a navy against the menace of Japan; that he, and he alone, had saved England from being humbled in the dust by Russia and France; that it had been *his* campaign plan that enabled England's Lord Roberts to defeat the Boers in South Africa; and so on and on.

No other such amazing words had ever fallen from the lips of a European king in peacetime within a hundred years. The entire continent buzzed with the fury of a hornet's nest. England was incensed. German statesmen were aghast. And in the midst of all this consternation, the kaiser became panicky and suggested to Prince von Bülow, the imperial chancellor, that he take the blame. Yes, he wanted von Bülow to announce that it was all his responsibility, that he had advised his monarch to say these incredible things.

"But Your Majesty," von Bülow protested, "it seems to me utterly impossible that anybody either in Germany or England could suppose me capable of having advised Your Majesty to say any such thing."

The moment those words were out of von Bülow's mouth,

he realized he had made a grave mistake. The Kaiser blew up.

"You consider me a donkey," he shouted, "capable of blunders you yourself could never have committed."

Von Bülow knew that he ought to have praised before he condemned; but since it was too late, he did the next best thing. He praised after he had criticized. And it worked a miracle.

"I'm far from suggesting that," he answered respectfully. "Your Majesty surpasses me in many respects; not only, of course, in naval and military knowledge, but above all, in natural science. I have often listened in admiration when Your Majesty explained the barometer, or wireless telegraphy, or the Roentgen rays. I am shamefully ignorant of all branches of natural science, have no notion of chemistry or physics, and am quite incapable of explaining the simplest of natural phenomena. But," von Bülow continued, "in compensation, I possess some historical knowledge and perhaps certain qualities useful in politics, especially in diplomacy."

The kaiser beamed. Von Bülow had praised him. Von Bülow had exalted him and humbled himself. The kaiser could forgive anything after that. "Haven't I always told you," he exclaimed with enthusiasm, "that we complete one another famously? We should stick together, and we will!"

He shook hands with von Bülow, not once, but several times. And later in the day he waxed so enthusiastic that he exclaimed with doubled fists, "If anyone says anything to me against Prince von Bülow, *I shall punch him in the nose.*"

Von Bülow saved himself in time—but, canny diplomat that he was, he nevertheless had made one error: he should have *begun* by talking about his own shortcomings and Wilhelm's superiority—not by intimating that the kaiser was a half-wit in need of a guardian.

If a few sentences humbling oneself and praising the other

party can turn a haughty, insulted kaiser into a staunch friend, imagine what humility and praise can do for you and me in our daily contacts. Rightly used, they will work veritable miracles in human relations.

Admitting one's own mistakes—even when one hasn't corrected them—can help convince somebody to change his or her behavior. This was illustrated more recently by Clarence Zerhusen of Timonium, Maryland, when he discovered his fifteen-year-old son was experimenting with cigarettes.

"Naturally, I didn't want David to smoke," Mr. Zerhusen told us, "but his mother and I smoked cigarettes; we were giving him a bad example all the time. I explained to Dave how I started smoking at about his age and how the nicotine had gotten the best of me and now it was nearly impossible for me to stop. I reminded him how irritating my cough was and how he had been after me to give up cigarettes not many years before. I didn't exhort him to stop or make threats or warn him about their dangers. All I did was point out how I was hooked on cigarettes and what it had meant to me.

"He thought about it for a while and decided he wouldn't smoke until he had graduated from high school. As the years went by David never did start smoking and has no intention of ever doing so.

"As a result of that conversation I made the decision to stop smoking myself, and with the support of my family, I have succeeded."

POINTS TO REMEMBER

1. To be able to criticize and not be hated for it, speak about your mistakes first.
2. Good leadership is to correct your subordinates without lowering their morale.
3. Sharing responsibility with others for their errors strengthens relationships.

13

THE HIGH COST OF GETTING EVEN

One night, years ago, as I was traveling through Yellowstone Park, I sat with other tourists on bleachers facing a dense growth of pine and spruce. Presently the animal which we had been waiting to see, the terror of the forests, the grizzly bear, strode out into the glare of the lights and began devouring the garbage that had been dumped there from the kitchen of one of the park hotels. A forest ranger, Major Martindale, sat on a horse and talked to the excited tourists about bears. He told us that the grizzly bear can whip any other animal in the Western world, with the possible exception of the buffalo and the Kadiak bear; yet I noticed that night that there was one animal, and only one, that the grizzly permitted to come out of the forest and eat with him under the glare of the lights: a skunk. The grizzly knew that he could liquidate a skunk with one swipe of his mighty paw. Why didn't he do it? Because he had found from experience that it didn't pay.

I found that out, too. As a farm boy, I trapped four-legged skunks along the hedgerows in Missouri; and, as a man, I encountered a few two-legged skunks on the sidewalks of New York. I have found from sad experience that it doesn't pay to stir up either variety.

When we hate our enemies, we are giving them power over

us: power over our sleep, our appetites, our blood pressure, our health, and our happiness. Our enemies would dance with joy if only they knew how they were worrying us, lacerating us, and getting even with us! Our hate is not hurting them at all, but our hate is turning our own days and nights into a hellish turmoil.

Who do you suppose said this: "If selfish people try to take advantage of you, cross them off your list, but don't try to get even. When you try to get even, you hurt yourself more than you hurt the other fellow?" …Those words sound as if they might have been uttered by some starry-eyed idealist. But they weren't. Those words appeared in a bulletin issued by the Police Department of Milwaukee.

How will trying to get even hurt you? In many ways. According to *Life* magazine, it may even wreck your health. "The chief personality characteristic of persons with hypertension [high blood pressure] is resentment," said *Life*. "When resentment is chronic, chronic hypertension and heart trouble follow."

So you see that when Jesus said, "Love your enemies," He was not only preaching sound ethics. He was also preaching twentieth-century medicine. When He said, "Forgive seventy times seven," Jesus was telling you and me how to keep from having high blood pressure, heart trouble, stomach ulcers, and many other ailments.

A friend of mine recently had a serious heart attack. Her physician put her to bed and ordered her to refuse to get angry about anything, no matter what happened. Physicians know that if you have a weak heart, a fit of anger *can* kill you. Did I say, *can* kill you? A fit of anger *did* kill a restaurant owner, in Spokane, Washington, a few years ago. I have in front of me now a letter from Jerry Swartout, chief of the police department, Spokane, Washington, saying: "A few years ago, William Falkaber, a man of sixty-eight who owned a café here in Spokane, killed himself by flying into a rage because his cook insisted on drinking coffee out of his saucer. The café owner was so indignant that he grabbed a revolver and started to chase the cook and fell dead from heart failure—with his hand still gripping the gun. The coroner's report declared that anger had caused the heart failure."

When Jesus said, "Love your enemies," He was also telling us how to improve our looks. I know women—and so do you—whose faces have been wrinkled and hardened by hate and disfigured by resentment. All the beauty treatments in Christendom won't improve their looks half so much as would a heart full of forgiveness, tenderness, and love.

Hatred destroys our ability to enjoy even our food. The Bible puts it this way: "Better is a dinner of herbs where love is, than a stalled ox and hatred therewith."

Wouldn't our enemies rub their hands with glee if they knew that our hate for them was exhausting us, making us tired and nervous, ruining our looks, giving us heart trouble, and probably shortening our lives?

Even if we can't love our enemies, let's at least love ourselves. Let's love ourselves so much that we won't permit our enemies to control our happiness, our health, and our looks. As Shakespeare put it:

> "Heat not a furnace for your foe so hot
> That it do singe yourself."

When Jesus said that we should forgive our enemies "seventy times seven," He was also preaching sound business. For example, I have before me as I write a letter I received from George Rona, Fradegata'n 24, Uppsala, Sweden. For years, George Rona was an attorney in Vienna; but during the Second

World War, he fled to Sweden. He had no money, needed work badly. Since he could speak and write several languages, he hoped to get a position as correspondent for some firm engaged in importing or exporting. Most of the firms replied that they had no need of such services because of the war, but they would keep his name on file...and so on. One man, however, wrote George Rona a letter saying: "What you imagine about my business is not true. You are both wrong and foolish. I do not need any correspondent. Even if I did need one, I wouldn't hire you because you can't even write good Swedish. Your letter is full of mistakes."

When George Rona read that letter, he was as mad as Donald Duck. What did this Swede mean by telling him he couldn't write the language! Why, the letter that this Swede himself had written was full of mistakes! So George Rona wrote a letter that was calculated to burn this man up. Then he paused. He said to himself, "Wait a minute, now. How do I know this man isn't right? I have studied Swedish, but it's not my native language, so maybe I do make mistakes I don't know anything about. If I do, then I certainly have to study harder if I ever hope to get a job. This man has possibly done me a favor, even though he didn't mean to. The mere fact that he expressed himself in disagreeable terms doesn't alter my debt to him. Therefore, I am going to write him and *thank* him for what he has done."

So George Rona tore up the scorching letter he had already written, and wrote another that said: "It was kind of you to go to the trouble of writing to me, especially when you do not need a correspondent. I am sorry I was mistaken about your firm. The reason that I wrote to you was that I made inquiry and your name was given to me as a leader in your field. I did not know I had made grammatical errors in my letter. I am sorry and ashamed of myself. I will now apply myself more diligently to the study of the Swedish language and try to correct my mistakes. I want to thank you for helping me get started on the road to self-improvement."

Within a few days, George Rona got a letter from this man, asking Rona to come to see him. Rona went—and got a job. George Rona discovered for himself that "a soft answer turneth away wrath."

We may not be saintly enough to love our enemies, but, for the sake of our own health and happiness, let's at least forgive them and forget them. That is the smart thing to do. "To be wronged or robbed," said Confucius, "is nothing unless you continue to remember it." I once asked General Eisenhower's son, John, if his father ever nourished resentments. "No," he replied, "Dad never wastes a minute thinking about people he doesn't like."

There is an old saying that a man is a fool who can't be angry, but a man is wise who won't be angry.

I was brought up in a family which read the Scriptures or repeated a verse from the Bible each night and then knelt down and said "family prayers." I can still hear my father, in a lonely Missouri farmhouse, repeating these words of Jesus—words that will continue to be repeated as long as man cherishes his ideals: "Love your enemies, bless them that curse you, do good to them that hate you, and pray for them which despitefully use you, and persecute you."

My father tried to live those words of Jesus; and they gave him an inner peace that the captains and the kings of earth have often sought for in vain.

POINTS TO REMEMBER

1. Hate works as a slow poison.
2. Love your enemies.
3. A man is a fool who can't be angry, but a man is wise who won't be angry.

14

THE SAFETY VALVE IN HANDLING COMPLAINTS

Most people trying to win others to their way of thinking do too much talking themselves. Let the other people talk themselves out. They know more about their business and problems than you do. So ask them questions. Let them tell you a few things.

If you disagree with them you may be tempted to interrupt. But don't. It is dangerous. They won't pay attention to you while they still have a lot of ideas of their own crying for expression. So listen patiently and with an open mind. Be sincere about it. Encourage them to express their ideas fully.

Does this policy pay in business? Let's see. Here is the story of a sales representative who was *forced* to try it.

One of the largest automobile manufacturers in the United States was negotiating for a year's requirements of upholstery fabrics. Three important manufacturers had worked up fabrics in sample bodies. These had all been inspected by the executives of the motor company, and notice had been sent to each manufacturer saying that, on a certain day, a representative from each supplier would be given an opportunity to make a final plea for the contract.

G.B.R., a representative of one manufacturer, arrived in town with a severe attack of laryngitis. "When it came my turn to meet the executives in conference," Mr. R— said as he related the story before one of my classes, "I had lost my voice. I could hardly whisper. I was ushered into a room and found myself face to face with the textile engineer, the purchasing agent, the director of sales and the president of the company. I stood up and made a valiant effort to speak, but I couldn't do anything more than squeak.

"They were all seated around a table, so I wrote on a pad of paper: 'Gentlemen, I have lost my voice. I am speechless.'

"'I'll do the talking for you,' the president said. He did. He exhibited my samples and praised their good points. A lively discussion arose about the merits of my goods. And the president, since he was talking for me, took the position I would have had during the discussion. My sole participation consisted of smiles, nods and a few gestures.

"As a result of this unique conference, I was awarded the contract, which called for over half a million yards of upholstery fabrics at an aggregate value of $ 1,600,000—the biggest order I had ever received.

"I know I would have lost the contract if I hadn't lost my voice, because I had the wrong idea about the whole proposition. I discovered, quite by accident, how richly it sometimes pays to let the other person do the talking."

Letting the other person do the talking helps in family situations as well as in business. Barbara Wilson's relationship with her daughter, Laurie, was deteriorating rapidly. Laurie, who had been a quiet, complacent child, had grown into an uncooperative, sometimes belligerent teenager. Mrs. Wilson lectured her, threatened her and punished her, but all to no avail.

"One day," Mrs. Wilson told one of our classes, "I just gave up. Laurie had disobeyed me and had left the house to visit her girl friend before she had completed her chores. When she returned I was about to scream at her for the ten-thousandth time, but I just didn't have the strength to do it. I just looked at her and said sadly, 'Why, Laurie, Why?'

"Laurie noted my condition and in a calm voice asked, 'Do you really want to know?' I nodded and Laurie told me, first hesitantly, and then it all flowed out. I had never listened to her. I was always telling her to do this or that. When she wanted to tell me her thoughts, feelings, ideas, I interrupted with more orders. I began to realize that she needed me—not as a bossy mother, but as a confidante, an outlet for all her confusion about growing up. And all I had been doing was talking when I should have been listening. I never heard her.

"From that time on I let her do all the talking she wanted. She tells me what is on her mind, and our relationship has improved immeasurably. She is again a cooperative person."

A large advertisement appeared on the financial page of a New York newspaper calling for a person with unusual ability and experience. Charles T. Cubellis answered the advertisement, sending his reply to a box number. A few days later, he was invited by letter to call for an interview. Before he called, he spent hours in Wall Street finding out everything possible about the person who had founded the business. During the interview, he remarked: "I should be mighty proud to be associated with an organization with a record like yours. I understand you started twenty-eight years ago with nothing but a desk room and one stenographer. Is that true?"

Almost every successful person likes to reminisce about his early struggles. This man was no exception. He talked for a long time about how he had started with $450 in cash and an original idea. He told how he had fought against discouragement and battled against ridicule, working Sundays and holidays, twelve to sixteen hours a day; how he had finally won against all odds until now the most important executives on Wall Street were coming to him for information and guidance. He was proud of such a record. He had a right to be, and he had a splendid time telling about it. Finally, he questioned Mr. Cubellis briefly about his experience, then called in one of his vice presidents and said: "I think this is the person we are looking for."

Mr. Cubellis had taken the trouble to find out about the accomplishments of his prospective employer, He showed an interest in the other person and his problems. He encouraged the other person to do most of the talking—and made a favorable impression.

Roy G. Bradley of Sacramento, California, had the opposite problem. He listened as a good prospect for a sales position talked himself into a job with Bradley's firm. Roy reported: "Being a small brokerage firm, we had no fringe benefits, such as hospitalization, medical insurance and pensions. Every representative is an independent agent. We don't even provide leads for prospects, as we cannot advertise for them as our larger competitors do.

"Richard Pryor had the type of experience we wanted for this position, and he was interviewed first by my assistant, who told him about all the negatives related to this job. He seemed slightly discouraged when he came into my office. I mentioned the one benefit of being associated with my firm, that of being an independent contractor and therefore virtually being self-employed.

"As he talked about these advantages to me, he talked himself out of each negative thought he had when he came in for the interview. Several times it seemed as though he was half talking to himself as he was thinking through each thought. At times I was tempted to add to his thoughts; however, as the interview came to a close I felt he had convinced himself very much on his own that he would like to work for my firm.

"Because I had been a good listener and let Dick do most of the talking, he was able to weigh both sides fairly in his mind, and he came to the positive conclusion, which was a challenge he created for himself. We hired him and he has been an outstanding representative for our firm."

Even our friends would much rather talk to us about their achievements than listen to us boast about ours.

La Rochefoucauld, the French philosopher, said: "If you want enemies, excel your friends; but if you want friends, let your friends excel you."

Why is that true? Because when our friends excel us, they feel important; but when we excel them, they—or at least some of them—will feel inferior and envious.

By far the best-liked placement counselor in the Midtown Personnel Agency in New York City was Henrietta G—. It hadn't always been that way. During the first few months of her association with the agency, Henrietta didn't have a single friend among her colleagues. Why? Because every day she would brag about the placements she had made, the new accounts she had opened and anything else she had accomplished.

"I was good at my work and proud of it," Henrietta told one of our classes. "But instead of my colleagues sharing my triumphs, they seemed to resent them. I wanted to be liked by these people. I really wanted them to be my friends. After listening to some of the suggestions made in this course, I started to talk about myself less and listen more to my associates. They also had things to boast about and were more excited about telling me about their accomplishments than about listening to my boasting. Now, when we have some time to chat, I ask them to share their joys with me, and I only mention my achievements when they ask."

POINTS TO REMEMBER

1. Ask the right questions.
2. Letting the other person do the talking helps in family situations as well as in business.
3. Encouraging the other person to do most of the talking makes a favorable impression.

15

NEVER WORRY ABOUT INGRATITUDE

I recently met a businessman in Texas who was burned up with indignation. I was warned that he would tell me about it within fifteen minutes after I met him. He did. The incident he was angry about had occurred eleven months previously, but he was still burned up about it. He couldn't talk of anything else. He had given his thirty-four employees ten thousand dollars in Christmas bonuses—approximately three hundred dollars each—and no one had thanked him. "I am sorry," he complained bitterly, "that I ever gave them a penny!"

"An angry man," said Confucius, "is always full of poison." This man was so full of poison that I honestly pitied him. He was about sixty years old. Now, life-insurance companies figure that, on the average, we will live slightly more than two thirds of the difference between our present age and eighty. So this man—if he was lucky—probably had about fourteen or fifteen years to live. Yet he had already wasted almost one of his few remaining years by his bitterness and resentment over an event that was past and gone. I pitied him.

Instead of wallowing in resentment and self-pity, he might have asked himself *why* he didn't get any appreciation. Maybe he had underpaid and overworked his employees. Maybe they considered a Christmas bonus not a gift, but something they had earned. Maybe he was so critical and unapproachable that no one dared or cared to thank him. Maybe they felt he gave the bonus because most of the profits were going for taxes anyway.

On the other hand, maybe the employees were selfish, mean, and ill-mannered. Maybe this. Maybe that. I don't know any more about it than you do. But I do know that Dr.. Samuel Johnson said:

"Gratitude is a fruit of great cultivation. You do not find it among gross people."

Here is the point I am trying to make: *this man made the human and distressing mistake of expecting gratitude.* He just didn't know human nature.

If you saved a man's life, would you expect him to be grateful? You might—but Samuel Leibowitz, who was a famous criminal lawyer before he became a judge, saved *seventy-eight* men from going to the electric chair! How many of these men, do you suppose, stopped to thank Samuel Leibowitz, or ever took the trouble to send him a Christmas card? How many? Guess… That's right—none.

Christ healed ten lepers in one afternoon—but how many of those lepers even stopped to thank Him? Only one. Look it up in Saint Luke. When Christ turned around to His disciples and asked, "Where are the other nine?" they had all run away. Disappeared without thanks! Let me ask you a question: Why should you and I—or this businessman in Texas—expect more thanks for our small favors than was given to Jesus Christ?

And when it comes to money matters! Well, that is even more hopeless. Charles Schwab told me that he had once saved a bank cashier who had speculated in the stock market with funds belonging to the bank. Schwab put up the money to save this man from going to the penitentiary. Was the cashier grateful? Oh, yes, for a little while. Then he turned against

Schwab and reviled him and denounced him—the very man who had kept him out of jail!

If you gave one of your relatives a million dollars, would you expect him to be grateful? Andrew Carnegie did just that. But if Andrew Carnegie had come back from the grave a little while later, he would have been shocked to find this relative cursing him! Why? Because Old Andy had left 365 million dollars to public charities—and had "cut him off with one measly million," as he put it.

That's how it goes. Human nature has always been human nature—and it probably won't change in your lifetime. So why not accept it? Why not be as realistic about it as was old Marcus Aurelius, one of the wisest men who ever ruled the Roman Empire. He wrote in his diary one day: "I am going to meet people today who talk too much—people who are selfish, egotistical, ungrateful. But I won't be surprised or disturbed, for I couldn't imagine a world without such people."

That makes sense, doesn't it? If you and I go around grumbling about ingratitude, who is to blame? Is it human nature—or is it our ignorance of human nature? Let's not expect gratitude. Then, if we get some occasionally, it will come as a delightful surprise. If we don't get it, we won't be disturbed.

Here is the first point I am trying to make in this chapter: It is natural for people to forget to be grateful; so, if we go around expecting gratitude, we are headed straight for a lot of heartaches.

I know a woman in New York who is always complaining because she is lonely. Not one of her relatives wants to go near her—and no wonder. If you visit her, she will tell you for hours what she did for her nieces when they were children: she nursed them through the measles and the mumps and the whooping cough; she boarded them for years; she helped to send one of them through business school, and she made a home for the other until she got married.

Do the nieces come to see her? Oh, yes, now and then, out of a spirit of duty. But they dread these visits. They know they will have to sit and listen for hours to half-veiled reproaches. They will be treated to an endless litany of bitter complaints and self-pitying sighs. And when this woman can no longer bludgeon, browbeat, or bully her nieces into coming to see her, she has one of her "spells." She develops a heart attack.

Is the heart attack real? Oh, yes. The doctors say she has "a nervous heart," suffers from palpitations. But the doctors also say they can do nothing for her—her trouble is emotional.

What this woman really wants is love and attention. But she calls it "gratitude." And she will never get gratitude or love, because she demands it. She thinks it's her due.

There are thousands of women like her, women who are ill from "ingratitude," loneliness, and neglect. They long to be loved; but the only way in this world that they can ever hope to be loved is to stop asking for it and to start pouring out love without hope of return.

Does that sound like sheer, impractical, visionary idealism? It isn't. It is just horse sense. It is a good way for you and me to find the happiness we long for. I know. I have seen it happen right in my own family. My own mother and father gave for the joy of helping others. We were poor—always overwhelmed by debts. Yet, poor as we were, my father and mother always managed to send money every year to an orphans' home. The Christian Home in Council Bluffs, Iowa. Mother and Father never visited that home. Probably no one thanked them for their gifts—except by letter—but they were richly repaid, for they had the joy of helping little children—without wishing for or expecting any gratitude in return.

After I left home, I would always send Father and Mother a

check at Christmas and urge them to indulge in a few luxuries for themselves. But they rarely did. When I came home a few days before Christmas, Father would tell me of the coal and groceries they had bought for some "widder woman" in town who had a lot of children and no money to buy food and fuel. What joy they got out of these gifts—the joy of giving without expecting anything whatever in return!

I believe my father would almost have qualified for Aristotle's description of the ideal man—the man most worthy of being happy. "The ideal man," said Aristotle, "takes joy in doing favors for others; but he feels ashamed to have others do favors for him. For it is a mark of superiority to confer a kindness; but it is a mark of inferiority to receive it."

Here is the second point I am trying to make in this chapter: If we want to find happiness, let's stop thinking about gratitude or ingratitude and give for the inner joy of giving.

HOW TO INCULCATE GRATITUDE IN CHILDREN

Parents have been tearing their hair about the ingratitude of children for ten thousand years.

Even Shakespeare's King Lear cried out, "How sharper than a serpent's tooth it is to have a thankless child!"

But why should children be thankful—unless we train them to be? Ingratitude is natural—like weeds. Gratitude is like a rose. It has to be fed and watered and cultivated and loved and protected.

If our children are ungrateful, who is to blame? Maybe we are. If we have never taught them to express gratitude to others, how can we expect them to be grateful to us?

I know a man in Chicago who has cause to complain of the ingratitude of his stepsons. He slaved in a box factory, seldom earning more than forty dollars a week. He married a widow, and she persuaded him to borrow money and send her two grown sons to college. Out of his salary of forty dollars a week, he had to pay for food, rent, fuel, clothes, and also for the payments on his notes. He did this for four years, working like a coolie, and never complaining.

Did he get any thanks? No; his wife took it all for granted—and so did her sons. They never imagined that they owed their step-father anything—not even thanks!

Who was to blame? The boys? Yes; but the mother was even more to blame. She thought it was a shame to burden their young lives with "a sense of obligation." She didn't want her sons to "start out under debt." So she never dreamed of saying: "What a prince your stepfather is to help you through college!" Instead, she took the attitude: "Oh, that's the least he can do."

She thought she was sparing her sons, but, in reality, she was sending them out into life with the dangerous idea that the world owed them a living. And it *was* a dangerous idea—for one of those sons tried to "borrow" from an employer, and ended up in jail!

We must remember that our children are very much what we make them. For example, my mother's sister—Viola Alexander, of 144 West Minnehaha Parkway, Minneapolis—is a shining example of a woman who has never had cause to complain about the "ingratitude" of children. When I was a boy, Aunt Viola took her own mother into her home to love and take care of; and she did the same thing for her husband's mother. I can still close my eyes and see those two old ladies sitting before the fire in Aunt Viola's farmhouse. Were they any "trouble" to Aunt Viola? Oh, often, I suppose. But you would never have guessed it from her attitude. She *loved* those old ladies—so she pampered them, and spoiled them, and made them feel at home. In addition, Aunt Viola had six children of her own; but it never occurred to her that she was doing anything especially noble, or deserved any halos for taking these old ladies into her home. To her, it was the natural thing, the right thing, the thing she wanted to do.

Where is Aunt Viola today? Well, she has now been a widow for twenty-odd years, and she has five grown-up children—five separate households—all clamoring to share her, and to have her come and live in their homes! Her children adore her; they never get enough of her. Out of "gratitude"? Nonsense! It is love—*sheer love.* Those children breathed in warmth and radiant human-kindness all during their childhoods. Is it any wonder that, now that the situation is reversed, they *give back* love?

So let us remember that to raise grateful children, we have to *be* grateful. Let us remember "little pitchers have big ears"— and watch what we say. To illustrate—the next time we are tempted to belittle someone's kindness in the presence of our children, let's stop. Let's never say: "Look at these dishcloths Cousin Sue sent for Christmas. She knit them herself. They didn't cost her a cent!" The remark may seem trivial to us—but the children are listening. So, instead, we had better say: "Look at the hours Cousin Sue spent making these for Christmas! Isn't she nice? Let's write her a thank-you note right now." And our children may unconsciously absorb the habit of praise and appreciation.

POINTS TO REMEMBER

1. An angry man is always full of poison.
2. Don't make the distressing mistake of expecting gratitude.
3. The only way to be loved is by stopping to ask for it.

16

WHEN NOTHING ELSE WORKS, TRY THIS

Charles Schwab had a mill manager whose people weren't producing their quota of work.

"How is it," Schwab asked him, "that a manager as capable as you can't make this mill turn out what it should?"

"I don't know," the manager replied. "I've coaxed the men, I've pushed them, I've sworn and cussed, I've threatened them with damnation and being fired. But nothing works. They just won't produce."

This conversation took place at the end of the day, just before the night shift came on. Schwab asked the manager for a piece of chalk, then, turning to the nearest man, asked:

"How many heats did your shift make today?"

"Six."

Without another word, Schwab chalked a big figure "6" on the floor, and walked away.

When the night shift came in, they saw the "6" and asked what it meant.

"The big boss was in here today," the day people said. "He asked us how many heats we made, and we told him six. He chalked it on the floor."

The next morning Schwab walked through the mill again. The night shift had rubbed out "6" and replaced it with a big "7".

When the day shift reported for work the next morning, they saw a big "7" chalked on the floor. So the night shift thought they were better than the day shift, did they? Well, they would show the night shift a thing or two. The crew pitched in with enthusiasm, and when they quit that night, they left behind them an enormous, swaggering "10". Things were stepping up

Shortly this mill, which had been lagging way behind in production, was turning out more work than any other mill in the plant.

The principle?

Let Charles Schwab say it in his own words: "The way to get things done," says Schwab, "is to stimulate competition. I do not mean in a sordid money-getting way, but in the desire to excel."

The desire to excel! The challenge! Throwing down the gauntlet! An infallible way of appealing to people of spirit.

Without a challenge, Theodore Roosevelt would never have been President of the United States. The Rough Rider, just back from Cuba, was picked for governor of New York State. The opposition discovered he was no longer a legal resident of the state, and Roosevelt, frightened, wished to withdraw. Then Thomas Collier Platt, then U.S. Senator from New York, threw down the challenge. Turning suddenly on Theodore Roosevelt, he cried in a ringing voice: "Is the hero of San Juan Hill a coward?"

Roosevelt stayed in the fight—and the rest is history. A challenge not only changed his life; it had a real effect upon the future of his nation.

"All men have fears, but the brave put down their fears and go forward, sometimes to death, but always to victory" was the motto of the King's Guard in ancient Greece. What greater challenge can be offered than the opportunity to overcome those fears?

When Al Smith was the governor of New York, he was up against it. Sing Sing, at the time the most notorious penitentiary west of Devil's Island, was without a warden. Scandals had been sweeping through the prison walls, scandals and ugly rumours. Smith needed a strong man to rule Sing Sing—an iron man. But who? He sent for Lewis E. Lawes of New Hampton.

"How about going up to take charge of Sing Sing?" he said jovially when Lawes stood before him. "They need a man up there with experience."

Lawes was flabbergasted. He knew the dangers of Sing Sing. It was a political appointment, subject to the vagaries of political whims. Wardens had come and gone—one lasted only three weeks. He had a career to consider. Was it worth the risk?

Then Smith, who saw his hesitation, leaned back in his chair and smiled. "Young fellow," he said, "I don't blame you for being scared. It's a tough spot. It'll take a big person to go up there and stay."

So he went. And he stayed. He stayed, to become the most famous warden of his time. His book *20,000 Years in Sing Sing* sold into the hundreds of thousands of copies. His broadcasts on the air and his stories of prison life have inspired dozens of movies. His "humanising" of criminals wrought miracles in the way of prison reform.

"I have never found," said Harvey S. Firestone, founder of the great Firestone Tyre and Rubber Company, "that pay and pay alone would either bring together or hold good people. I think it was the game itself."

Frederic Herzberg, one of the great behavioral scientists, concurred. He studied in depth the work attitudes of thousands of people ranging from factory workers to senior executives. What do you think he found to be the most motivating factor—the one facet of the jobs that was most stimulating? Money? Good working conditions? Fringe benefits? No—not any of those. The one major factor that motivated people was the work itself. If the work was exciting and interesting, the worker looked forward to doing it and was motivated to do a good job.

That is what every successful person loves: the game. The chance for self-expression. The chance to prove his or her worth, to excel, to win. That is what makes foot-races, and hog-calling, and pie-eating contests. The desire to excel. The desire for a feeling of importance.

POINTS TO REMEMBER

1. The way to get things done is by stimulating competition.
2. The desire to excel is essential to actually succeed.
3. Your work should be your biggest motivation.

17

HOW TO CURE MELANCHOLY IN FOURTEEN DAYS

Here is the most astonishing statement that *I* ever read from the pen of a great psychiatrist. This statement was made by Alfred Adler. He used to say to his melancholia patients: "You can be cured in fourteen days if you follow this prescription. Try to think every day how you can please someone."

That statement sounds so incredible that I feel I ought to try to explain it by quoting a couple of pages from Dr. Adler's splendid book, *What Life Should Mean to You*.

"Melancholia," says Adler on page 258 of *What Life Should Mean to You:*

Melancholia is like a long-continued rage and reproach against others, though for the purpose of gaining care, sympathy and support, the patient seems only to be dejected about his own guilt. A melancholiac's first memory is generally something like this: "I remember I wanted to lie on the couch, but my brother was lying there. I cried so much that he had to leave."

Melancholiacs are often inclined to revenge themselves by committing suicide, and the doctor's first care is to avoid giving them an excuse for suicide. I myself try to relieve the whole tension by proposing to them, as the first rule in treatment, "Never do anything you don't like." This seems to be very modest, but I believe that it goes to the root of the whole trouble. If a melancholiac is able to do anything he wants, whom can he accuse? What has he got to revenge himself for? "If you want to go to the theater," I tell him, "or to go on a holiday, do it. If you find on the way that you don't want to, stop it." It is the best situation any one could be in. It gives a satisfaction to his striving for superiority. He is like God and can do what he pleases. On the other hand, it does not fit very easily into his style of life. He wants to dominate and accuse others and if they agree with him there is no way of dominating them. This rule is a great relief and I have never had a suicide among my patients…

Generally the patient replies, "But there is nothing I like doing." I have prepared for this answer, because I have heard it so often. "Then refrain from doing anything you dislike," I say. Sometimes, however, he will reply, "I should like to stay in bed all day." I know that, if I allow it, he will no longer want to do it. I know that, if I hinder him, he will start a war. I always agree.

This is one rule. Another attacks their style of life still more directly. I tell them, "You can *be* cured in fourteen days if you follow this prescription. Try to think every day *how* you can please some one." See what this means to them. They are occupied with the thought, "How can I worry some one." The answers are very interesting. Some say, "This will be very easy for me. I have done it all my life." They have never done it. I ask them to think it over. They do not think it over. I tell them, "You can make use of all the time you spend when you are unable to go to sleep by thinking how you can please some one, and it will be a big step forward in your health." When I see them next day, I ask them, "Did you think over what I suggested?" They answer, "Last night I went to sleep as soon as I got into bed. All this must be done, of course, in a modest, friendly manner, without a hint of superiority.

Others will answer, "I could never do it. "I am so worried." I tell them, "Don't stop worrying; but at the same time you can think now and then of others". I want to direct their interest always towards their fellows. Many say, "Why should I please others? Others do not try to please me." "You must think of your health," I answer. "The others will suffer later on." It is extremely rare that I have found a patient who said, "I have thought over what you suggested." All my efforts are devoted towards increasing the social interest of the patient. I know that the real reason for his malady is his lack of co-operation and I want him to see it too. As soon as he can connect himself with his fellow men on an equal and co-operative footing, he is cured... The most important task imposed by religion has always been "Love thy neighbor."... It is the individual who is not interested in his fellow man who has the greatest difficulties in life and provides the greatest injury to others. It is from among such individuals that all human failures spring... All that we demand of a human being, and the highest praise we can give him, is that he should be a good fellow worker, a friend to all other men, and a true partner in love and marriage.

Dr. Adler urges us to do a good deed every day. And what is a good deed? "A good deed," said the prophet Mohammed, "is one that brings a smile of joy to the face of another."

Why will doing a good deed every day produce such astounding effects on the doer? Because trying to please others will cause us to stop thinking of ourselves: the very thing that produces worry and fear and melancholia.

POINTS TO REMEMBER

1. Try to think how you can please someone every day.
2. Never do anything you don't like.
3. Do a good deed daily to have positive mindset.

18

IF YOU MUST FIND FAULT, THIS IS THE WAY TO BEGIN

A friend of mine was a guest at the White House for a weekend during the administration of Calvin Coolidge. Drifting into the President's private office, he heard Coolidge say to one of his secretaries, "That's a very pretty dress you are wearing this morning, and you are a very attractive young woman."

That was probably the most effusive praise Silent Cal had ever bestowed upon a secretary in his life. It was so unusual, so unexpected, that the secretary blushed in confusion. Then Coolidge said, "Now, don't get stuck up. I just said that to make you feel good. From now on, I wish you would be a little more careful with your punctuation."

His method was probably a bit obvious, but the psychology was superb. It is always easier to listen to unpleasant things after we have heard some praise of our good points.

A barber lathers a man before he shaves him; and that is precisely what McKinley did back in 1896, when he was running for President. One of the prominent Republicans of that day had written a campaign speech that he felt was just a trifle better than Cicero and Patrick Henry and Daniel Webster all rolled into one. With great glee, this chap read his immortal speech aloud to McKinley. The speech had its fine points, but it just wouldn't do. McKinley didn't want to hurt the man's feelings. He must not kill the man's splendid enthusiasm, and yet he had to say "no". Note how adroitly he did it.

"My friend, that is a splendid speech, a magnificent speech," McKinley said. "No one could have prepared a better one. There are many occasions on which it would be precisely the right thing to say, but is it quite suitable to this particular occasion? Sound and sober as it is from your standpoint, I must consider its effect from the party's standpoint. Now go home and write a speech along the lines I indicate, and send me a copy of it."

He did just that. McKinley blue-pencilled and helped him rewrite his second speech, and he became one of the effective speakers of the campaign.

Here is the second most famous letter that Abraham Lincoln ever wrote. (His most famous one was written to Mrs. Bixby, expressing his sorrow for the death of the five sons she had lost in battle.) Lincoln probably dashed this letter off in five minutes; yet it sold at public auction in 1926 for $12,000, and that, by the way, was more money than Lincoln was able to save during half a century of hard work. The letter was written to General Joseph Hooker on 26 April 1863, during the darkest period of the Civil War. For eighteen months, Lincoln's generals had been leading the Union Army from one tragic defeat to another. Nothing but futile, stupid human butchery. The nation was appalled. Thousands of soldiers had deserted from the army, and even the Republican members of the Senate had revolted and wanted to force Lincoln out of the White House. "We are now on the brink of destruction," Lincoln said. "It appears to me that even the Almighty is against us. I can hardly see a ray of hope." Such was the period of black sorrow and chaos out of which this letter came.

I am printing the letter here because it shows how Lincoln tried to change an obstreperous general when the very fate of the nation could have depended upon the general's action.

This is perhaps the sharpest letter Abe Lincoln wrote after he became President; yet you will note that he praised General Hooker before he spoke of his grave faults.

Yes, they were grave faults, but Lincoln didn't call them that. Lincoln was more conservative, more diplomatic. Lincoln wrote: "There are some things in regard to which I am not quite satisfied with you." Talk about tact! And diplomacy!

Here is the letter addressed to General Hooker:

I have placed you at the head of the Army of the Potomac. Of course, I have done this upon what appears to me to be sufficient reasons, and yet I think it best for you to know that there are some things in regard to which I am not quite satisfied with you.

I believe you to be a brave and skillful soldier, which, of course, I like. I also believe you do not mix politics with your profession, in which you are right. You have confidence in yourself, which is a valuable if not an indispensable quality.

You are ambitious, which, within reasonable bounds, does good rather than harm. But I think that during General Burnside's command of the army you have taken counsel of your ambition and thwarted him as much as you could, in which you did a great wrong to the country and to a most meritorious and honorable brother officer.

I have heard, in such a way as to believe it, of your recently saying that both the army and the Government needed a dictator. Of course, it was not for this, but in spite of it, that I have given you command.

Only those generals who gain successes can set up as dictators. What I now ask of you is military success and I will risk the dictatorship.

The Government will support you to the utmost of its ability, which is neither more nor less than it has done and will do for all commanders. I much fear that the spirit which you have aided to infuse into the army, of criticizing their commander and withholding confidence from him, will now turn upon you. I shall assist you, as far as I can, to put it down.

Neither you nor Napoleon, if he were alive again, could get any good out of an army while such spirit prevails in it, and now beware of rashness. Beware of rashness, but with energy and sleepless vigilance, go forward and give us victories.

You are not a Coolidge, a McKinley or a Lincoln. You want to know whether this philosophy will operate for you in everyday business contacts. Will it? Let's see. Let's take the case of W.P. Gaw, of the Wark Company, Philadelphia.

The Wark Company had contracted to build and complete a large office building in Philadelphia by a certain specified date. Everything was going along well; the building was almost finished, when suddenly the subcontractor making the ornamental bronze work to go on the exterior of this building declared that he couldn't make delivery on schedule. What! An entire building held up! Heavy penalties! Distressing losses! All because of one man!

Long-distance telephone calls. Arguments! Heated conversations! All in vain. Then Mr. Gaw was sent to New York to beard the bronze lion in his den.

"Do you know you are the only person in Brooklyn with

your name?" Mr. Gaw asked the president of the subcontracting firm shortly after they were introduced. The president was surprised. "No, I didn't know that."

"Well," said Mr. Gaw, "when I got off the train this morning, I looked in the telephone book to get your address, and you're the only person in the Brooklyn phone book with your name."

"I never knew that," the subcontractor said. He checked the phone book with interest. "Well, it's an unusual name," he said proudly. "My family came from Holland and settled in New York almost two hundred years ago." He continued to talk about his family and his ancestors for several minutes. When he finished that, Mr. Gaw complimented him on how large a plant he had and compared it favorably with a number of similar plants he had visited. "It is one of the cleanest and neatest bronze factories I ever saw," said Gaw.

"I've spent a lifetime building up this business," the subcontractor said, "and I am rather proud of it. Would you like to take a look around the factory?"

During this tour of inspection, Mr. Gaw complimented the other man on his system of fabrication and told him how and why it seemed superior to those of some of his competitors. Gaw commented on some unusual machines, and the subcontractor announced that he himself had invented those machines. He spent considerable time showing Gaw how they operated and the superior work they turned out. He insisted on taking his visitor to lunch. So far, mind you, not a word had been said about the real purpose of Gaw's visit.

After lunch, the subcontractor said, "Now, to get down to business. Naturally, I know why you're here. I didn't expect that our meeting would be so enjoyable. You can go back to Philadelphia with my promise that your material will be fabricated and shipped, even if other orders have to be delayed."

Mr. Gaw got everything that he wanted without even asking for it. The material arrived on time, and the building was completed on the day the completion contract specified.

Would this have happened had Mr. Gaw used the hammer-and-dynamite method generally employed on such occasions?

Dorothy Wrublewski, a branch manager of the Fort Monmouth, New Jersey, Federal Credit Union, reported to one of our classes how she was able to help one of her employees become more productive.

"We recently hired a young lady as a teller trainee. Her contact with our customers was very good. She was accurate and efficient in handling individual transactions. The problem developed at the end of the day when it was time to balance out.

"The head teller came to me and strongly suggested that I fire this woman. 'She is holding up everyone else because she is so slow in balancing out. I've shown her over and over, but she can't get it. She's got to go.' The next day I observed her working quickly and accurately when handling the normal everyday transactions, and she was very pleasant with our customers.

"It didn't take long to discover why she had trouble balancing out. After the office closed, I went over to talk with her. She was obviously nervous and upset. I praised her for being so friendly and outgoing with the customers and complimented her for the accuracy and speed used in that work. I then suggested we review the procedure we use in balancing the cash drawer. Once she realized I had confidence in her, she easily followed my suggestions and soon mastered this function. We have had no problems with her since then.'

Beginning with praise is like the dentist who begins his work with Novocain. The patient still gets a drilling, but the Novocain is pain-killing.

POINTS TO REMEMBER

1. It is always easier to listen to unpleasant things after we have heard some praise of our good points.
2. There are a thousand ways to say "no."
3. Your trust is the best gift you can give to someone.

19

A DROP OF HONEY

If your temper is aroused and you tell 'em a thing or two, you will have a fine time unloading your feelings. But what about the other person? Will he share your pleasure? Will your belligerent tones, your hostile attitude, make it easy for him to agree with you?

"If you come at me with your fists doubled," said Woodrow Wilson, "I think I can promise you that mine will double as fast as yours; but if you come to me and say, 'Let us sit down and take counsel together, and, if we differ from each other, understand why it is that we differ, just what the points at issue are,' we will presently find that we are not so far apart after all, that the points on which we differ are few and the points on which we agree are many, and that if we only have the patience and the candor and the desire to get together, we will get together."

Nobody appreciated the truth of Woodrow Wilson's statement more than John D. Rockefeller Jr. Back in 1915, Rockefeller was the most fiercely despised man in Colorado. One of the bloodiest strikes in the history of American industry had been shocking the state for two terrible years. Irate, belligerent miners were demanding higher wages from the Colorado Fuel and Iron Company; Rockefeller controlled that company. Property had been destroyed, troops had been called out. Blood had been shed. Strikers had been shot, their bodies riddled with bullets.

At a time like that, with the air seething with hatred, Rockefeller wanted to win the strikers to his way of thinking. And he did it. How? Here's the story. After weeks spent in making friends, Rockefeller addressed the representatives of the strikers. This speech, in its entirety, is a masterpiece. It produced astonishing results. It calmed the tempestuous waves of hate that threatened to engulf Rockefeller. It won him a host of admirers. It presented facts in such a friendly manner that the strikers went back to work without saying another word about the increase in wages for which they had fought so violently.

The opening of that remarkable speech follows. Note how it fairly glows with friendliness. Rockefeller, remember, was talking to men who, a few days previously, had wanted to hang him by the neck to a sour apple tree; yet he couldn't have been more gracious, more friendly if he had addressed a group of medical missionaries. His speech was radiant with such phrases as I am *proud* to be here, having *visited* in *your homes*, met many of your wives and children, we meet here not as strangers, but *as friends*…spirit of *mutual friendship*, our *common interests*, it is only by *your courtesy* that I am here.

"This is a red-letter day in my life," Rockefeller began. "It is the first time I have ever had the good fortune to meet the representatives of the employees of this great company, its officers and superintendents, together, and I can assure you that I am proud to be here, and that I shall remember this gathering as long as I live. Had this meeting been held two weeks ago, I should have stood here a stranger to most of you, recognizing a few faces, I having had the opportunity last week of visiting all the camps in the southern coal field and of talking individually with practically all of the representatives, except those who were away; having visited in your homes, met many of your wives and children, we meet here not as strangers, but as friends, and it is in that spirit of mutual friendship that I am glad to have this opportunity to discuss with you our common interests.

"Since this is a meeting of the officers of the company and the representatives of the employees, it is only by your courtesy that I am here, for I am not so fortunate as to be either one or the other; and yet I feel that I am intimately associated with you men, for, in a sense, I represent both the stockholders and the directors."

Isn't that a superb example of the fine art of making friends out of enemies?

Suppose Rockefeller had taken a different tack. Suppose he had argued with those miners and hurled devastating facts in their faces. Suppose he had told them by his tones and insinuations that they were wrong. Suppose that, by all the rules of logic, he had proved that they were wrong. What would have happened? More anger would have been stirred up, more hatred, more revolt.

If a man's heart is rankling with discord and ill feeling toward you, you can't win him to your way of thinking with all the logic in Christendom. Scolding parents and domineering bosses and husbands and nagging wives ought to realize that people don't want to change their minds. They can't be forced or driven to agree with you or me. But they may possibly be led to, if we are gentle and friendly, ever so gentle and ever so friendly.

Lincoln said that, in effect, over a hundred years ago. Here are his words:

It is an old and true maxim that "a drop of honey catches more flies than a gallon of gall." So with men, if you would win a man to your cause, first convince him that you are his sincere friend. Therein is a drop of honey that catches his heart; which, say what you will, is the great high road to his reason.

HOW TO HANDLE FAILURES

A member of one of our classes, Gerald H. Winn of Littleton, New Hampshire, reported how by using a friendly approach, he obtained a very satisfactory settlement on a damage claim.

"Early in the spring," he reported, "before the ground had thawed from the winter freezing, there was an unusually heavy rainstorm and the water, which normally would have run off to nearby ditches and storm drains along the road, took a new course onto a building lot where I had just built a new home.

"Not being able to run off, the water pressure built up around the foundation of the house. The water forced itself under the concrete basement floor, causing it to explode, and the basement filled with water. This ruined the furnace and the hot-water heater. The cost to repair this damage was in excess of $2,000. I had no insurance to cover this type of damage.

"However, I soon found out that the owner of the subdivision had neglected to put in a storm drain near the house which could have prevented this problem. I made an appointment to see him. During the 25-mile trip to his office, I carefully reviewed the situation and, remembering the principles I learned in this course, I decided that showing my anger would not serve any worthwhile purpose. When I arrived, I kept very calm and started by talking about his recent vacation to the

West Indies; then, when I felt the timing was right, I mentioned the 'little' problem of water damage. He quickly agreed to do his share in helping to correct the problem.

"A few days later he called and said he would pay for the damage and also put in a storm drain to prevent the same thing from happening in the future.

"Even though it was the fault of the owner of the sub-division, if I had not begun in a friendly way, there would have been a great deal of difficulty in getting him to agree to the total liability."

Years ago, when I was a barefoot boy walking through the woods to a country school out in Northwest Missouri, I read a fable about the sun and the wind. They quarrelled about which was the stronger, and the wind said, "I'll prove I am. See the old man down there with a coat? I bet I can get his coat off him quicker than you can."

So the sun went behind a cloud, and the wind blew until it was almost a tornado, but the harder it blew, the tighter the old man clutched his coat to him.

Finally, the wind calmed down and gave up, and then the sun came out from behind the clouds and smiled kindly on the old man. Presently, he mopped his brow and pulled off his coat. The sun then told the wind that gentleness and friendliness were always stronger than fury and force.

The use of gentleness and friendliness is demonstrated day after day by people who have learnt that a drop of honey catches more flies than a gallon of gall.

POINTS TO REMEMBER

1. The art of making friends out of enemies.
2. The most appreciated speech is one which is friendly in its tone.
3. A drop of honey catches more flies than a gallon of gall.

20

ACHIEVING BALANCE

Monsignor Tom Hartman has been a priest for more than twenty years. His whole life is dedicated to the service of God and others. His days consist of consoling the needy, ministering to the sick, advising the distraught, and trying to bring people closer to God. But one thing was sadly missing from the monsignor's busy days.

One morning his father phoned at the rectory. In those days Hartman was assigned to St. James Parish in Seaford, Long Island. His father owned a liquor store down the road in Farmingdale. In all his years of growing up and in all his time as a priest, Hartman could never remember his parents saying anything negative about him. But on the phone that morning, his father's voice had a slightly irritated tone.

"Tom, I'd like to sit down and talk with you about something," his father said.

"Sure," Hartman told him, and the two men made a date.

When they finally got together, his father spoke immediately about what was on his mind. "Tom," he said, "your mother and I admire you. We're always hearing about the good work you are doing, and we're very proud of you. But I think you're overlooking your family. I understand you've got to help a lot of people in your life, but many of those people are going to come and go. Your family will always be there for you. And what's happened is, when you call us, you're always asking us to do something for you. You just seem too busy to take the time to talk."

Hartman was momentarily taken aback. "Well, Dad," he said, "when I was growing up, I watched you. You were in the produce business working seventy hours a week. And I have to say I admired you. So you know, I've tried to do the same."

But his father didn't sound convinced. "What you don't see, Tom, is that your work is harder than mine was," he said. "Mine was physical. It was fruit and produce. And then I would come home and be present with my family." Hartman didn't know what to say, and he felt relieved when his father said he wasn't really looking for any instant response. "I just want you to think about this," his father said.

Hartman was disturbed enough by the conversation to cancel the rest of his appointments for the day. Then he decided to call his brothers and sisters. He described later what he discovered on the phone. "When I called them," he said, "we were into the conversation about three or four minutes, and every one of them said almost the exact same thing: 'What do you want?' That's when I had to admit that my father was right."

Even a man whose calling is to maintain perspective and balance needed to have someone remind him that—in one part of his life, at least—he wasn't practicing what he preached. That's a mistake everyone makes from time to time.

It is vital for all of us to balance out our lives, to make room for things other than work. This won't only produce happier and more satisfying personal lives. Almost inevitably, it will also make people more energetic, more focused, and more productive at work.

Walter A. Green, the chairman of Harrison Conference Services, likens a balanced, productive life to a "several-legged stool." Too many people, Green believes, have only a single dimension to their lives. They are focused round the clock on their careers.

"In my experience, all too often, this one-dimensional perspective continues throughout one's life," Green says. "What I would urge is that your life be a several-legged stool, with a dimension for your family, another for your friends, your avocations, your health. I have seen many examples of people in their thirties, forties, and fifties whose professions or careers did not materialize as they had expected. This spells trouble for those whose lives have been a one-legged stool."

This is a problem even for highly successful people. "At some stage in your life," Green continues, "you will want something else. It is possible to begin to develop friendships and interests after middle age. But watch a fifty-year-old learn to ride a bicycle for the first time!" It's not a graceful sight.

The importance of balance—to individuals and to the companies that employ them—is only now being fully understood. But well-led companies everywhere are trying to help their people put true balance into their lives.

At the New York City headquarters of Tiger Management Corporation, a worldwide money-management firm, a fully equipped workout room has been installed right outside the president's office. All Tiger employees are encouraged to use it.

"The gym is going to be tripled in size," Tiger president Julian H. Robertson, Jr., says proudly. "I find the young people all seem to come here after work. The fact that they are here rather than at health clubs all over the city is a tremendous boon for us. They are talking with each other. They are exchanging ideas. All that is really good for us." And obviously it's good for them too—physically and mentally.

"I don't think it's possible to be a great manager or a great executive without being a total person," says Andrés Navarro, president of SONDA, S.A., a Chilean computer-systems company that does business in North and South America. Navarro has an apt analogy. "If you want to be an athlete, maybe to throw the javelin, it's not enough to have the strongest arm. You need the whole body to be strong."

And if you want to be a great leader, you need all parts of your life to be strong and intact. "You see," explains Navarro, "a good executive who makes great decisions and makes money in the company but doesn't get along with his wife, his children, and other people in general is missing a crucial part of life. If you want to grow and be a good leader, you've got to be a complete man—or a complete woman. And the most important part of it is your family."

Richard Fenstermacher of the Ford Motor Company promotes the very same idea among his employees. "We tell our people, 'Your lives are two-dimensional,'" Fenstermacher says. "If you find all of your identity at Ford, that's going to be a problem because you have a responsibility to your family as well."

Undeniably, most modern leaders don't achieve a perfect balance all of the time. The many balls that are being juggled aren't easy to keep aloft. The usual tendency for ambitious people is to put the business first. It just seems so much more urgent, so much more pressing, so much more crucial.

Fred Sievert at New York Life has a different set of pressures on his time, but he admits candidly that he too finds it hard to manage all the competing interests in his life. "I'm struggling every day to bring balance into my life," he says. "I could literally spend all my waking hours at work and a year from now not know everything I'd like to know. It's very difficult."

Yes, it is. Attaining a reasonable division of time between work and leisure "is the greatest challenge," believes Ray Stata, of Analog Devices, Inc. But it's worth the effort to master the challenge.

HAPPY WIFE, HAPPY LIFE

John B. Robinson, Jr., of Fleet Financial Group, Inc., has realized the benefits that come with having a happy home life. "There has never been any doubt in my mind what's most important to me," says Robinson. A big title? Salary? Stock options? A country home? "What's most important to me, long-term, is myself, my wife, and my family." What does this mean in practice? "I try to keep a sense of what's fair and what's equitable, and if I've been giving too much to the job and not enough to the family, I say, 'I'm not going to do that. I'm not going to say yes to that dinner, and I'm not going to shortchange my family life.'"

Most people, if they were asked directly, would probably echo Robinson's sentiments. Family is more important. Time to play is essential. But most people don't put that concept into action. They don't treat balance as a top priority. They fall into the habit of responding to the immediate pressure of work and ignoring the immediate and long-term pleasure that flows from having a satisfying personal life.

After his revelation about his family life, Monsignor Tom Hartman taught himself how to "waste" time. "I try in my life for an hour a day to do nothing," Hartman explains. "I waste time with God, with people, with nature, my job. It has transformed my eyes. Now I see the connection we have to each other. It is so important not to force things but to appreciate them." Appreciate your family, your friends, your environment, yourself, whatever it is that gets your mind off work.

At Michael and Nancy Crom's home outside San Diego, Saturdays are always reserved for that. As Nancy grabs a few last minutes of sleep, Michael and daughter Nicole make pancakes, Nicole's favorite meal. The two of them go out to the garden, where they check on the strawberry plants, water the flowers, and feed the birds. He tells her stories from the life of Nicky-Nicole and Belinda McIntosh, the make-believe characters the two of them have invented.

"We do that every Saturday, whether I've been traveling or I've been in the office," Michael says. "Watching the joy in her eyes keeps me joyful too."

Wolfgang Schmitt of Rubbermaid takes a walk with his family most nights. "It would be unusual if we didn't go out for a walk," Schmitt explains. "If our older sons are there, they go with us. The little guy always goes with us because he lives at home. We go out for forty minutes, an hour, whatever, just walking around. We do it no matter what the weather."

Schmitt also makes a point of spending time alone. "Just physically doing something is therapy. Raking leaves, cutting wood, planting trees. Any chore is therapeutic."

Bill Makahilahila at SGS-Thomson makes time for himself every day—even though it means getting up at three o'clock in the morning. Makahilahila explains his practice of predawn rising: "I'm busy all day. I'm usually here until seven or eight in the evening, and I know I need to be here in the morning. I don't know why, but I've just gotten to the point where I am in deep meditation in the mornings. It's so quiet, I can stretch myself, be creative, read, or reflect on my day."

The benefits are immediate. "When I've done that," he says, "I begin to have peace of mind and self-confidence, even in the midst of the deepest problems that I know I'm going to have to face that day."

Corning's David Luther runs. He also vacations with his wife and son four times a year, skiing or beachcombing. He makes sure he reads things that have nothing to do with work, and when all else fails, "I just go out and sit on the deck and watch the hawks."

Once you've analyzed how to enjoy your leisure time, bring some of that same spirit into work. Who ever said the office has to be a depressing place?

Certainly not Richard Fenstermacher of the Ford Motor Company. Fenstermacher recalls doing business with a company that brought that spirit of levity right into the executive suite.

"When they bring somebody on the board," explains Fenstermacher, "they give the new person a Mickey Mouse watch. There's a big presentation out of the office. Everybody comes and stands around, and somebody gives a speech. The thing is, you don't have to spend twenty-five years with this company to get a watch. Here's your watch. When you look at that watch, we want to remind you to have fun when you work. That's why it's Mickey Mouse."

Tom Saunders makes enjoyment a high priority at his international merchant bank, Saunders Karp & Company. "We waste time. When we've got a little bit of time to sit around, we laugh at each other about something or make fun of each other. I make fun of them all the time and they make fun of me worse. But all the time I'm ragging them, all the time. We have good times. We don't take ourselves too seriously."

Television newsman Hugh Downs has borrowed Churchill's time-tested method of workday relaxation and given it his own special spin. "The one thing I have in common with great people—only one thing—is that I can sleep for very short periods and be refreshed," says Downs. "I can sit down in a chair and go to sleep for three minutes, five minutes, and wake up and it's like I've had a night's sleep. I would go into my dressing room often when I was otherwise all ready and say, 'Wake me two minutes before air time,' And they'd come in and wake me two minutes before air. I'd go out and do the show.

"My wife laughs at that," Downs continues. "She says, 'If you were condemned to death in two hours, you're going before the firing squad in two hours, you'd take a nap the first hour and face the problem the second hour.' It's probably true. If there were nothing I could do about it in that first hour, it would be appropriate to take a nap."

What is always appropriate—at the office, at home, on the road, wherever you happen to find yourself—is to keep real balance in your life. As Fleet Financial's John Robinson says, "There are many ways of getting involved in outside activities. Every time you get involved in outside interests, it adds balance—whether it's church-related, civic-related, or school-related. I just try to avoid extremes, I guess."

Singer-songwriter Neil Sedaka had two close friends growing up in Brooklyn, a young couple who had great ambition in their lives but also just loved to have a good time. Over the years they both achieved tremendous professional and financial success, but they lost something along the way. It was the balance they once knew in their lives. Sedaka wrote a song about his friends, which turned into a giant hit. The song was called "The Hungry Years."

"They struggled to hit the top," Sedaka recalls. "Success and money. But when they finally did it, they discovered that they missed the times when they were just getting started, when they were hanging out in the old neighborhood, when they were building a life together.

"It's like, 'I want that five-million-dollar home.' But then you finally hit it, you actually get to move in, and after a couple of months, you say, 'Is this all? Is this it?' You miss those years that you did things together. You've lost some of the pleasure and balance in your life." There's nothing wrong with material success, but that alone is not enough to sustain a happy life.

How can you start balancing your life? The first step is to change your attitude. You've got to stop thinking of time for your family, for exercise, or for leisure as wasted time. Achievers often feel they need to apologize for leisure time. Try to rid yourself of that thought. Relaxation is not a dirty word.

This leads to the second step in the process: you have to make time for leisure activity. Most of us are overcommitted. Perhaps it's time to reevaluate priorities. Make a decision to devote as much energy to planning your leisure time as you devote to planning your workday.

The third step is to act. Do something. Get involved in activities that are not work-related. They will leave you happier, healthier, more focused, and as a result, a better leader.

CONSISTENTLY HIGH PERFORMANCE COMES FROM A BALANCE BETWEEN WORK AND LEISURE.

POINTS TO REMEMBER

1. Attaining a balanced life is more productive and satisfying.
2. Only a good person can be a good leader.
3. Achieving a reasonable balance between work and leisure is the greatest challenge.